Life After Estrangement

A Guide for Parents Cut Off by Adult Children and A

Compassionate Roadmap to Grief, Growth, and Letting Go

Without Giving Up Hope

Nicci Brochard
&
Dr. Ben Chuba

Life After Estrangement

A Guide for Parents Cut Off by Adult Children and A

Compassionate Roadmap to Grief, Growth, and Letting Go

Without Giving Up Hope

CROSSBORDER

New York, London, Quebec

Contents

Introduction 1

Chapter 1: The Unspoken Grief – When Your Child Walks Away . 4

Introduction 4
Understanding Estrangement as a Form of Ambiguous Loss 5
Why It Hurts So Deeply: Parental Identity, Expectations, and Emotional Rupture . 6
The Silence Around Estrangement in Society and Its Hidden Toll 8
Conclusion 9

Chapter 2: How Did We Get Here? – Triggers, Patterns, and

Shifting Boundaries 11

Introduction 11
Common Causes and Triggers: Perceived Injustices, Boundaries, Past Trauma 12
Family Dynamics and Intergenerational Wounds 14
The Rise of "Cutting Off" in the Age of Therapy, Autonomy, and Social Media ... 16
Conclusion 17

Chapter 3: It's Not Just You – Understanding the Estrangement

Epidemic 19

Introduction 19
Statistics and Rising Trends in Family Estrangement 20
Cultural Shifts Around Boundaries, Self-Care, and "Toxic" Labels 21
The Double Bind: Damned If You Stay Close, Damned If You Step Back 24
Conclusion 26

Chapter 4: The Rollercoaster of Emotions – Shame, Anger, Guilt,

and Sadness 27

Introduction 27
The Unique Emotional Terrain of Estranged Parents 28
Why Guilt and Shame Often Sabotage Healing 30
Journaling, Therapy, and Safe Ways to Process Deep Emotional Pain 32
Conclusion 34

Chapter 5: Rewriting the Story – Breaking the Loop of Blame and Self-Doubt 35

Introduction 35
Understanding Narrative Grief and Emotional Storytelling 36
Reframing Your Parental Role in a Changed Relationship 37
From "I Failed" to "We Were All Doing the Best We Could" 39
Conclusion 41

Chapter 6: Letting Go Without Giving Up – The Art of Hopeful Surrender 43

Introduction 43
What It Means to Let Go of Control Without Letting Go of Love 44
Healthy Detachment: Not Coldness, But Boundaries with Grace 45
How to Live with Open Hands Instead of Clinging Fists 48
Conclusion 50

Chapter 7: Messages Left Unsent – When Communication Breaks Down 51

Introduction 51
Should You Write a Letter? When Silence Says More 52
Navigating the Temptation to "Explain Yourself" vs. Respecting Space 54
Scripts and Tools for Non-Invasive, Open-Hearted Outreach 56
Conclusion 58

Chapter 8: Navigating Holidays, Birthdays, and Family Gatherings 60

Introduction 60
How to Handle Grief Flare-Ups During Major Events 61
Creating New Rituals and Traditions That Honor Healing 63
Dealing with Other Family Members Who "Take Sides" or Avoid the Topic 65
Conclusion 67

Chapter 9: Rebuilding a Life – Identity Beyond Parenthood 69

Introduction 69
Reclaiming Your Wholeness as a Human Being 70
Finding Meaning, Community, and Purpose Outside the Parental Role 72
Exploring Passions, Friendships, and Spiritual Connection 74

Conclusion 75

Chapter 10: When Estrangement Ends – Reunions, Relapses, and Redefinitions 77

Introduction 77
If Reconciliation Happens: What to Expect, What to Avoid 78
Trust-Building in Fragile Reunions 80
Accepting New Boundaries Without Needing to "Go Back to How It Was" 82
Conclusion 84

Chapter 11: Staying Connected to Love – Even Without Contact 85

Introduction 85
Practicing Unconditional Love from a Distance 86
Rituals, Prayers, and Quiet Acts of Continued Care 88
Love That Expects Nothing in Return – But Always Leaves the Light On 91
Conclusion 92

Chapter 12: Helping Others Understand – Navigating Judgment and Isolation 94

Introduction 94
Dealing with Societal Shame and Misunderstanding 95
How to Respond to Awkward Questions and "Helpful" Advice 97
Joining or Creating Support Groups for Estranged Parents 99
Conclusion 101

Chapter 13: Your Life, Still Beautiful – Peace, Meaning, and the Long View 103

Introduction 103
Grief and Joy Can Coexist 104
What Your Journey Teaches Others About Grace and Endurance 105
Embracing Life Fully – Scars, Strength, and All 107
Conclusion 109

Epilogue 110

Introduction

Estrangement between parents and their adult children is an incredibly painful experience, one that leaves emotional scars and creates a complex, often isolating journey. For parents, the anguish of being cut off by their children can feel like an unexplainable and overwhelming loss. Whether it's a matter of communication breakdowns, emotional conflicts, or other life circumstances, the silence from the children they raised can be excruciating. The grief that comes with estrangement is not just the loss of a relationship, but also a rupture of dreams and hopes, leaving parents in a state of confusion, heartache, and emotional turmoil.

"Life After Estrangement" is a heartfelt guide designed specifically for parents who find themselves in this very situation. This book offers not only understanding of the emotional complexities that come with estrangement but also practical advice on how to navigate the painful journey of healing. It is a resource for parents who feel they are walking alone in their grief, offering a roadmap through the emotional landscape of estrangement with compassion and insight.

In the chapters that follow, parents will find validation for their feelings, reassurance that they are not alone, and actionable steps to move through their grief without giving up hope. Estrangement is often misunderstood by those who haven't experienced it. People may offer well-meaning but sometimes unhelpful advice, such as "just move on" or "it's only a phase," dismissing the depth of the pain felt by parents. This book aims to bridge that gap by creating a space for parents to acknowledge their pain, understand their emotions, and begin a path to healing that is uniquely their own.

The emotional journey of estrangement can feel like a rollercoaster— one filled with guilt, anger, confusion, and, at times, profound self-doubt. It's easy for parents to question where they went wrong or wonder if they failed as parents. Many will cycle through feelings of hope and despair, seeking answers or hoping for reconciliation, but unsure of how to approach the situation. This book dives into the emotional grief that estranged parents experience, from the initial shock to the eventual realization that there may not be a quick resolution. It discusses the importance of understanding the emotional undercurrents of estrangement, particularly how to process feelings of guilt, betrayal, and deep loss.

However, "Life After Estrangement" is not just a book about pain. It is about growth, self-discovery, and the potential for personal transformation even in the face of adversity. Estrangement, as difficult as it is, can offer parents the opportunity to redefine themselves and their lives. It challenges them to grow beyond their role as parents and embrace new ways of thinking, living, and relating to themselves and others. This book explores ways to reconnect with one's inner strength, cultivate self-compassion, and find new meaning in life after the loss of a child's presence.

At its core, the message of this book is about letting go—letting go of the need for control over the relationship, letting go of the expectations, and learning how to release the toxic emotions that can hold parents captive. Letting go doesn't mean giving up hope. It means finding peace with what is and embracing the possibility of moving forward in a healthy, positive way. Parents will learn how to create space for their own emotional healing while holding onto hope that reconciliation, whether with their children or within themselves, is still possible.

Throughout "Life After Estrangement," parents will be encouraged to find new ways to cope with the emotional pain, to reframe their situation, and to explore the possibility of growth and peace in their own lives. The journey through estrangement may not be one that parents choose, but it is one that can lead to profound healing, self-empowerment, and ultimately, a new understanding of love, resilience, and hope.

Whether parents are at the beginning of their estrangement, in the midst of it, or years into it, this book offers guidance, comfort, and hope for the road ahead.

Nicci and I (Ben) thank you for choosing our book. We promise you will find it helpful. Thank you.

Chapter 1

The Unspoken Grief – When Your Child Walks Away

Introduction

For many parents, one of the most unimaginable experiences is the moment when their child decides to walk away—when the relationship with the very person they nurtured, loved, and raised unravels. It is a grief unlike any other, one that doesn't fit neatly into society's typical understanding of loss. There are no funeral arrangements, no public mourning, no clear markers of finality. The loss is ambiguous, drawn out, and agonizingly silent. Yet, it is very real. The hurt, the confusion, and the pain that accompany estrangement are profound and life-altering.

In this chapter, we will explore the complexities of estrangement as a form of ambiguous loss—a type of grief that often goes unacknowledged by both the estranged parents and the society at large. We will delve into why estrangement hurts so deeply, examining how it touches the very core of a parent's identity, the weight of unmet expectations, and the emotional rupture that accompanies the severing of a once-cherished bond. Finally, we will look at the silence surrounding estrangement in our society and how this silence compounds the toll it takes on parents, often leaving them to suffer in isolation.

Understanding Estrangement as a Form of Ambiguous Loss

The term "ambiguous loss" was first coined by psychologist Pauline Boss, who defined it as a loss that lacks closure or clear understanding. Estrangement, in this sense, is a perfect example of ambiguous loss because the parent's grief is marked by uncertainty and confusion. In a typical bereavement, there is an event—the death of a loved one—that allows people to process their grief. The situation is clear: the person is gone, and there is a definite finality to it. But in the case of estrangement, the situation is murkier. The child may still be alive, but the parent's connection to them is severed or deeply strained. There is no closure, no ritual to help with the mourning, and no definitive understanding of what went wrong.

Estrangement, particularly between parents and adult children, can arise for many reasons. It may be the result of a conflict, a difference of values, or a breakdown in communication. It can occur suddenly, or it may develop slowly over time, with small misunderstandings escalating into deep-rooted resentment. Regardless of how it begins, the parent is left in a state of limbo. They may not fully understand why their child has distanced themselves, and they may never get the answers they need to fully comprehend the situation. This lack of closure is one of the defining characteristics of ambiguous loss, making it uniquely difficult to navigate emotionally.

Parents who experience estrangement are not only grieving the absence of their child from their lives but are also forced to contend with the deep questions about their role as parents and the worth of the relationships they have invested in for years. They may feel a constant, gnawing uncertainty about what the future holds—whether reconciliation is possible or if they will have to live with this painful reality for the rest of their lives.

Why It Hurts So Deeply: Parental Identity, Expectations, and Emotional Rupture

When a child walks away, it strikes at the very heart of a parent's identity. Parents often define themselves through their relationships with their children. From the moment of conception, a parent's life becomes entwined with their child's journey—from the first steps to the first day of school, from the teenage years to adulthood. This bond becomes a central part of the parent's self-image. They see themselves not just as individuals, but as caregivers, nurturers, and providers. The role of a parent is so integral to their sense of self that when that relationship fractures or disintegrates, it can feel like a personal loss of self-worth.

This emotional rupture can be likened to the loss of a part of oneself. The parent may experience intense feelings of rejection and confusion as they try to understand how the relationship deteriorated. The expectation that the parent-child relationship will evolve over time, as children grow and mature into adults, often blindsides the parent when that relationship suddenly ends or is strained beyond repair. The rupture is not just about the loss of communication; it is about the disintegration of an emotional connection that once defined much of the parent's emotional life.

Parents often carry high hopes and expectations for their relationship with their children. They imagine a future where they are present at their child's wedding, hold their grandchild in their arms, and offer guidance and love in their later years. These expectations are built over a lifetime, woven into the fabric of family traditions, holidays, and daily routines. When estrangement occurs, those dreams and hopes are shattered. Parents are left with a sense of emptiness, having envisioned a future that now seems out of reach. They may feel anger and resentment towards their child for causing this disruption in their life, or they may feel guilty, wondering if they are to blame for the breakdown of the relationship.

In many cases, the emotional pain of estrangement can feel like an invisible wound. On the outside, parents may appear to be functioning normally—going about their daily lives, attending social gatherings, or continuing with their work. But inside, the pain is all-consuming. It can manifest as anxiety, depression, insomnia, or physical symptoms like headaches or stomachaches. The emotional toll is severe, and the lack of a clear cause or resolution often exacerbates these feelings.

Furthermore, estrangement can make parents feel like failures in the most intimate and personal sense. In a world where parenting is often viewed through a lens of success or failure, the parent who faces estrangement from their child may feel a deep sense of shame. They may wonder why they couldn't do more, or what they could have done differently to prevent the breakdown. The shame is compounded by the fact that estrangement is often seen as a taboo subject in many social circles. Parents who experience estrangement may feel a sense of isolation, ashamed to discuss their feelings with friends or family for fear of judgment or misunderstanding.

The Silence Around Estrangement in Society and Its Hidden Toll

Estrangement is a silent, isolating experience, often shrouded in stigma and shame. While other forms of loss—like the death of a loved one—are publicly acknowledged and supported by friends and family, estrangement can leave parents feeling as though they are carrying an invisible burden. Society tends to offer little support for those going through this type of grief, and there are few cultural rituals or social norms to help guide them through the mourning process.

In many cases, estranged parents suffer in silence, unable to talk openly about their pain. They may fear judgment from others, who may blame them for the breakdown of the relationship or view them as unfit parents. The absence of social recognition for estrangement can exacerbate feelings of loneliness and isolation. Friends and family may not know how to provide support, or they may avoid the topic altogether, out of discomfort or lack of understanding.

This silence can take a toll on the parent's mental health. Without the opportunity to process their grief or share their pain, they may feel emotionally stifled, carrying their grief in secret. There may also be a sense of shame attached to estrangement—especially if the parent feels they have somehow failed their child or contributed to the estrangement. This silence and lack of support can prolong the grieving process, making it harder for parents to heal and move forward.

There is also a societal tendency to minimize the pain of estrangement. People may suggest that the parent simply "move on," or that "it's just a phase." While well-meaning, these suggestions are often dismissive of the deep emotional toll that estrangement takes. The reality is far more complex. For many parents, the loss is permanent, and the emotional scars can last for years. Ignoring the gravity of the situation or minimizing the pain only deepens the wound, making it harder for the parent to find closure or peace.

In the absence of open discussion or recognition, parents may feel unheard, as though their grief is invisible. This can lead to a sense of being trapped in their own pain, without any clear way out. The silence around estrangement not only prolongs the grief but also reinforces feelings of shame, rejection, and isolation.

Conclusion

Estrangement is a deeply painful and often misunderstood experience. It is a grief that is invisible to the outside world, yet profound for those who live through it. The loss is ambiguous, the reasons unclear, and the path to healing uncertain. The emotional rupture that occurs when a child walks away from their parent touches the core of parental identity, unearths unfulfilled expectations, and leaves a lasting wound that is difficult to mend.

In a society that often fails to acknowledge the depth of this pain, estranged parents are left to grieve in silence, with few opportunities to express their sorrow or find support. Yet, understanding estrangement as a form of ambiguous loss can provide clarity and insight into the complex emotional landscape that parents must navigate. Recognizing the deep, multifaceted hurt that comes with estrangement is the first step in healing and reclaiming hope.

The journey through estrangement is one that is uniquely personal, but it is also shared by many. By acknowledging the grief and pain associated with estrangement, parents can begin to heal, rebuild their sense of self, and, ultimately, find peace. While estrangement may change the relationship with a child, it does not have to define the parent's life. Through self-compassion, support, and a willingness to face the emotional realities of estrangement, parents can move forward into a future filled with growth, resilience, and, eventually, healing.

Chapter 2

How Did We Get Here? – Triggers, Patterns, and Shifting Boundaries

Introduction

Estrangement is rarely a singular event. It is often the result of a series of complex, interconnected factors that build over time. For many parents, the moment of estrangement—the "cut off" that may seem abrupt—can feel like an emotional ambush. Yet, when viewed in the broader context of family dynamics, past trauma, shifting boundaries, and societal changes, it becomes clear that estrangement often follows patterns, even if those patterns were not immediately visible.

In this chapter, we will explore the common causes and triggers of estrangement, from perceived injustices to the breaking of boundaries and the impact of unresolved past trauma. We will dive into family dynamics, examining the intergenerational wounds that may be passed down through generations, influencing the relationships between parents and their adult children. Additionally, we will consider the rise of the concept of "cutting off" in contemporary society, particularly within the context of therapy, autonomy, and social media. By understanding these triggers and patterns, parents may begin to gain insight into how they arrived at this painful place—and what, if anything, they can do to heal.

Common Causes and Triggers: Perceived Injustices, Boundaries, Past Trauma

Estrangement does not usually happen in a vacuum. In many cases, it is the culmination of unresolved issues, misunderstandings, and perceived injustices. These elements often create an emotional storm that leads to distance, if not complete estrangement.

1. **Perceived Injustices**: One of the most common triggers of estrangement is a sense of injustice. For adult children, this might manifest as a feeling of being misunderstood, mistreated, or unsupported by their parents. These perceived injustices may stem from childhood experiences that were not properly addressed or acknowledged. For example, a parent may have unknowingly belittled their child's feelings, disregarded their emotional needs, or failed to protect them from external harm. Over time, the accumulation of these unresolved grievances can lead to a breaking point, where the child feels that they must distance themselves in order to protect their emotional well-being.

   For parents, the perception of injustice may come in the form of a lack of gratitude, disrespect, or perceived abandonment by their child. Parents may feel that they have given everything for their children—providing love, stability, and guidance—and yet receive little in return. This sense of unreciprocated effort can lead to feelings of bitterness, resentment, and ultimately, a breakdown in communication.

12

2. **Boundaries**: Boundaries—both healthy and unhealthy—play a crucial role in the development of estrangement. Boundaries are the limits that we set in relationships to protect our emotional and psychological well-being. When boundaries are violated, ignored, or misunderstood, it can cause significant emotional damage.

   In the case of estranged parents, it is often the crossing of boundaries—whether intentional or not—that leads to conflict. Perhaps a parent oversteps by trying to control aspects of their child's life, such as their career, relationships, or parenting style. On the other hand, a child may feel that their parent is constantly encroaching on their privacy, belittling their choices, or not respecting their independence. When these boundaries are repeatedly violated, the child may feel forced to cut ties in order to preserve their own sense of autonomy and self-respect.

   Similarly, parents may find themselves dealing with the erosion of their own boundaries, as children demand more time, attention, or support than they can give. Parents who struggle with setting healthy boundaries may end up feeling emotionally drained and resentful, which can strain the relationship to the point of estrangement.

3. **Past Trauma**: The seeds of estrangement can often be traced back to unresolved trauma from both the parent's and the child's past. For parents, this may include experiences from their own childhoods, where they were raised in environments where

emotional needs were ignored or not met. Parents may bring these unconscious patterns into their own families, perpetuating cycles of neglect or emotional distance.

For children, past trauma may include feelings of neglect, emotional or physical abuse, or an inability to bond with the parent in a meaningful way. These early experiences can leave emotional scars that carry into adulthood. When these wounds remain unaddressed, they can surface as deep-seated resentment or anger toward the parent, often manifesting as estrangement.

The pain of past trauma can often be buried beneath years of surface-level interactions. However, as children grow older and develop the capacity to reflect on their experiences, they may start to see their relationships with their parents through a more critical lens. This newfound awareness can trigger emotional upheaval, which may culminate in estrangement as a means of self-protection.

Family Dynamics and Intergenerational Wounds

To fully understand the causes of estrangement, it is essential to look at family dynamics and the intergenerational wounds that often influence parent-child relationships. Family dynamics are a complex web of interactions, roles, expectations, and histories. When these dynamics are unhealthy or dysfunctional, they can set the stage for estrangement.

1. **Role Expectations**: Parents often enter relationships with their children with certain expectations about the roles they will play

in each other's lives. These expectations can be based on cultural norms, personal desires, or unresolved issues from the parent's own childhood. For example, a parent may expect that their adult children will take on a caregiving role as they age, while the child may have their own vision of independence and autonomy. When these expectations clash, it can create a power struggle that leads to emotional distance.

Similarly, the roles that children are expected to play within the family—whether that be the responsible one, the peacemaker, or the rebellious one—can create tension. Parents who impose rigid expectations on their children may inadvertently stifle their growth, leading to resentment that manifests later in life as estrangement.

2. **Intergenerational Wounds**: Often, the seeds of estrangement are planted long before the child becomes an adult. These seeds are part of a broader pattern of intergenerational wounds. Parents may carry emotional baggage from their own families that influences the way they interact with their children. For example, a parent who was raised in an environment where emotional expression was repressed may struggle to communicate openly with their child, leading to misunderstandings and emotional distance.

These intergenerational wounds can be passed down through unspoken expectations, unacknowledged trauma, and learned behaviors. Children who grow up in such environments may find it difficult to form healthy attachments, leading to strained relationships with their parents. Over time, these unresolved wounds can contribute to estrangement as both parties struggle to break free from the emotional patterns they have inherited.

The Rise of "Cutting Off" in the Age of Therapy, Autonomy, and Social Media

In recent years, the concept of "cutting off" has gained increasing visibility, especially in the context of therapy and social media. The notion of "cutting off" is often framed as a way of protecting one's emotional health by severing toxic or harmful relationships. For many individuals, therapy has become an essential tool for understanding their emotional needs, setting boundaries, and learning how to assert their autonomy.

In the age of therapy, there is a growing emphasis on individual empowerment and self-care. People are increasingly encouraged to prioritize their mental health and well-being, even if it means distancing themselves from relationships that are harmful. For some adult children, this means cutting ties with a parent whom they perceive as emotionally damaging or toxic. Therapy provides a framework for understanding these dynamics, and in some cases, estrangement is seen as a necessary step toward healing.

At the same time, social media has played a significant role in shaping modern relationships. Social platforms like Facebook, Instagram, and Twitter offer instant access to people's lives, but they also present a curated, often idealized version of reality. The pressure to present a perfect image of family life can heighten feelings of inadequacy or resentment when things go wrong. Social media also provides an avenue for comparison, where individuals can compare their relationships to those of others. For adult children, seeing other people's seemingly perfect parent-child relationships can deepen feelings of anger, jealousy, or inadequacy, potentially leading to estrangement.

Furthermore, social media offers a space for individuals to share their experiences with estrangement publicly, contributing to the normalization of cutting off toxic relationships. While this can provide a sense of validation for those experiencing estrangement, it can also create a culture of "cutting off" as a quick fix, rather than fostering open dialogue and reconciliation.

The rise of autonomy and therapy in contemporary society has made estrangement a more visible and accepted choice, especially for younger generations. While this shift has empowered individuals to take control of their emotional health, it has also added a layer of complexity to family relationships, particularly when estrangement occurs unexpectedly or without sufficient understanding of the underlying emotional dynamics.

Conclusion

Estrangement is not a simple or one-dimensional issue. It is a deeply layered experience that often arises from a combination of personal, familial, and societal factors. From perceived injustices and boundary violations to past trauma and intergenerational wounds, the roots of estrangement can be traced back to a wide range of influences. As society shifts toward greater individualism, autonomy, and therapy-driven solutions, the practice of "cutting off" has become more normalized, adding new dimensions to the way we understand family relationships.

In order to navigate estrangement, it is essential to understand the triggers and patterns that lead to it. Parents and children alike must recognize that estrangement does not happen in isolation—it is often the culmination of years of complex interactions, unmet needs, and unresolved emotional wounds. By examining these factors, parents can begin to understand how they arrived at this difficult place and begin to take the first steps toward healing, whether that involves reconciling, setting new boundaries, or coming to terms with the reality of their situation. The path to healing begins with understanding, and by gaining insight into the triggers, patterns, and societal shifts that contribute to estrangement, both parents and children can begin to move forward, with or without reconciliation.

Chapter 3

It's Not Just You – Understanding the Estrangement Epidemic

Introduction

For many parents dealing with estrangement, it can feel like an isolated experience, as though they are the only ones facing such a painful and bewildering situation. The emotional turmoil of being cut off by a child can make one feel alone in their grief, as if no one truly understands the depths of the heartbreak. However, the reality is that family estrangement is far more common than most people realize. In recent years, there has been a significant rise in the number of families experiencing estrangement, especially between parents and adult children. This trend, which has become more widely discussed in recent years, has led to what can be described as an "estrangement epidemic," affecting countless families worldwide.

In this chapter, we will explore the rising trends and statistics surrounding family estrangement, examine the cultural shifts that have contributed to this phenomenon, and delve into the complexities of the "double bind" faced by estranged parents. We will also consider how changes in societal attitudes toward boundaries, self-care, and the labeling of relationships as "toxic" have created new challenges for family dynamics. By understanding the broader context of estrangement, parents can better understand that they are not alone, and that their pain is shared by many others.

Statistics and Rising Trends in Family Estrangement

While family estrangement has always existed, its prevalence has grown in recent years. According to studies, estrangement between parents and their adult children is becoming more widespread. Research conducted by the University of Denver found that nearly 27% of parents in the U.S. reported being estranged from one or more of their children. This number has been steadily increasing, as more families are faced with the reality of adult children cutting ties with their parents.

The reasons behind this rise in estrangement are varied and complex. Some studies suggest that the increase in estrangement is linked to greater societal changes, such as the rise in individualism, the normalization of therapy and self-care, and the growing trend of prioritizing personal well-being. These shifts have led to a cultural environment where emotional boundaries are more easily recognized and enforced, often resulting in family members severing ties when relationships are perceived as unhealthy or toxic.

In addition to these cultural shifts, there has also been an increase in the acknowledgment of emotional abuse and mistreatment within families. While such issues may have been dismissed or overlooked in the past, they are now being recognized as legitimate reasons for estrangement. As society becomes more aware of the effects of toxic relationships, more individuals are willing to confront the dynamics within their families, which sometimes leads to the difficult decision to sever ties.

One significant factor in the rising trend of estrangement is the impact of social media. With the advent of online platforms, people are now able to easily share their personal experiences, including those related to family dynamics. This has led to greater visibility of estrangement, as individuals who may have once felt isolated now see that others are experiencing similar situations. The increased visibility of estrangement may contribute to the normalization of cutting off family members, with some viewing it as a form of self-protection or emotional liberation.

While estrangement is a deeply painful experience for parents, it is essential to understand that it is not a rare phenomenon. The growing statistics and trends in family estrangement reflect a larger cultural shift in how families are structured and how relationships are navigated. Parents dealing with estrangement should take comfort in knowing that they are not alone, and that this experience is increasingly common in today's society.

Cultural Shifts Around Boundaries, Self-Care, and "Toxic" Labels

In recent decades, there has been a profound cultural shift regarding the concepts of boundaries, self-care, and what constitutes a "toxic" relationship. These changes have had a significant impact on family dynamics, particularly with regard to estrangement. The growing emphasis on emotional boundaries, self-care, and mental health has provided individuals with the tools and language to recognize and address unhealthy relationships within their families.

1. **Boundaries**: The concept of boundaries has become central to many conversations around mental health and personal well-being. As therapy has gained prominence in mainstream culture, people have become more attuned to the importance of setting and maintaining healthy boundaries in their relationships. Boundaries are seen as essential for preserving emotional well-being, and many individuals now prioritize protecting themselves from emotional harm.

   For adult children, this focus on boundaries has led to a greater awareness of when a relationship with a parent feels stifling, controlling, or damaging. When parents overstep emotional boundaries—by being too demanding, intrusive, or critical—adult children may feel that cutting ties is the only way to preserve their autonomy and sense of self. Conversely, parents may feel that their attempts to maintain a close connection with their children are being rejected or misunderstood, which can lead to feelings of helplessness and confusion.

2. **Self-Care**: The rise of self-care as a cultural movement has also played a role in the rise of estrangement. Self-care, which includes prioritizing one's emotional, physical, and mental health, has become an essential practice for many people. The focus on self-care has encouraged individuals to make decisions that are in their

best interest, even if those decisions involve distancing themselves from toxic or unhealthy relationships.

For estranged adult children, the decision to cut off a parent may be framed as an act of self-care—a necessary step in taking control of their emotional health. They may see their parent as an emotional burden, a source of stress, or a person who continuously triggers negative feelings. In this context, estrangement can be viewed as an empowered choice to safeguard one's emotional well-being. However, from the parent's perspective, this decision can feel like an unjust rejection and can bring about intense feelings of loss, anger, and grief.

3. **Toxic Labels**: The growing use of the term "toxic" to describe harmful relationships has also contributed to the rise in family estrangement. In today's discourse around emotional health, people are more likely to label relationships as toxic when they feel that certain behaviors or patterns are causing harm. The label "toxic" is used to describe relationships where there is emotional abuse, manipulation, control, or neglect, and it has become more widely accepted to sever ties with individuals who are seen as toxic.

    For adult children, this label can be a powerful justification for estrangement. If a parent's behavior is seen as emotionally damaging, the decision to cut them off can be framed as an act of self-preservation. However, this label can also be problematic. In some cases, the "toxic" label may be applied to a relationship without fully understanding the nuances of the dynamics involved. It can also be used to justify extreme measures without considering the potential for reconciliation or healing.

Parents, on the other hand, may find themselves labeled as toxic by their children, which can be deeply painful. They may feel that their actions were misinterpreted or that they were unfairly criticized. The rise of the "toxic" label can create an atmosphere in which relationships are easily discarded without addressing the underlying issues or seeking resolution.

The Double Bind: Damned If You Stay Close, Damned If You Step Back

One of the most painful aspects of estrangement is the double bind that parents often find themselves in. On the one hand, they may feel compelled to stay close to their children, even if the relationship is strained or unhealthy. On the other hand, they may feel that stepping back is the only way to preserve their emotional health and avoid further conflict. This emotional tug-of-war can leave parents feeling trapped and uncertain about how to proceed.

1. **Damned If You Stay Close**: For many parents, staying close to their estranged children can feel like an emotional rollercoaster. They may constantly try to repair the relationship, reaching out in hopes of reconciliation, but are met with silence or rejection. The continued attempts to stay close can lead to emotional exhaustion, as parents struggle to balance their desire for connection with the reality of being rejected. In some cases,

parents may compromise their own emotional well-being in an attempt to appease their children, sacrificing their own mental health in the process.

Moreover, staying close to a child who is emotionally distant can be damaging. It may result in the parent feeling constantly undermined, criticized, or unloved, leading to deep emotional scars. However, parents often feel a sense of obligation to remain in contact, believing that their love and support will eventually heal the rift. This belief can keep them emotionally invested, even when the relationship seems beyond repair.

2. **Damned If You Step Back**: On the other hand, parents who decide to step back from the relationship may feel as though they are abandoning their child, even if the decision is made out of necessity. The fear of being accused of neglect or failure as a parent can weigh heavily on them. Stepping back may feel like giving up, and it can be seen as an admission of defeat. Parents may feel that distancing themselves is a betrayal, but they may also feel that it is the only way to protect their own emotional health.

The double bind becomes even more complex when parents are faced with societal pressure to maintain close familial ties. In many cultures, there is a strong emphasis on family unity, and estrangement is often viewed as a failure or a shameful event. Parents may feel caught between the desire to honor family expectations and the need to protect themselves from further harm. This pressure can make the decision to step back feel like an impossible choice.

Conclusion

Estrangement is a complex and increasingly widespread issue that is influenced by a variety of factors, including shifting cultural norms, changing family dynamics, and personal well-being. As societal attitudes toward boundaries, self-care, and the labeling of relationships as toxic continue to evolve, the rise in family estrangement has become an undeniable epidemic. Parents who experience estrangement are not alone in their pain, as rising statistics reveal the growing prevalence of this issue.

The cultural shifts that have contributed to estrangement, including the emphasis on boundaries and self-care, have empowered individuals to protect their emotional health by severing harmful relationships. However, these shifts also complicate family dynamics and create a double bind for parents who feel torn between staying close to their estranged children and stepping back to preserve their own well-being.

By understanding the broader cultural and societal forces that contribute to estrangement, parents can gain perspective on their situation. Estrangement is not a personal failure but a reflection of the changing ways in which relationships are navigated and maintained in today's world. Parents must remember that while the path to healing may be long and difficult, they are not alone in their journey. The estrangement epidemic is a shared experience that, when understood, can lead to greater empathy and resilience.

Chapter 4

The Rollercoaster of Emotions – Shame, Anger, Guilt, and Sadness

Introduction

Estrangement is not merely an event or a series of actions—it is an emotional journey. The moment a parent is cut off by their child, it is as though they are thrown onto a turbulent rollercoaster of feelings. From the shock and disbelief of the initial estrangement to the recurring waves of shame, guilt, anger, and sadness, the emotional terrain of estranged parents is incredibly complex. Each day can bring a new challenge, a new wave of overwhelming emotion, and an uncertain future. The deep emotional pain that parents experience is not just the result of losing a child—it's also the result of the internal struggle that arises as they try to make sense of what went wrong, why they feel so rejected, and what they could have done differently.

In this chapter, we will explore the unique emotional experience of estranged parents, focusing on the most common feelings that surface: guilt, shame, anger, and sadness. We will also delve into why guilt and shame can be particularly sabotaging to the healing process and how these emotions, if not addressed, can keep parents stuck in a cycle of pain. Finally, we will explore practical ways for parents to process their deep emotional pain in a healthy way—through journaling, therapy, and other safe methods—so that they can begin the long process of healing.

The Unique Emotional Terrain of Estranged Parents

Estrangement is one of the most emotionally complex experiences a parent can endure. Unlike other types of loss, such as death or divorce, estrangement comes with layers of unresolved feelings, unanswered questions, and a lack of closure. The emotional journey is long and unpredictable, with no clear path forward. Parents may feel like they are constantly riding an emotional rollercoaster, with ups and downs, twists and turns, and moments of deep despair followed by fleeting moments of hope.

1. **Shock and Disbelief**: The initial shock of estrangement is often the first and most overwhelming emotion parents experience. It's as though the rug has been pulled out from under them, and they are left grappling with a sense of disbelief that their child has cut them off. Parents may ask themselves, "How could this have happened?" or "What did I do wrong?" In the early stages, this disbelief can be all-consuming, and parents may find it difficult to accept the reality of the situation.

2. **Guilt**: Guilt is perhaps the most prevalent emotion experienced by estranged parents. They often feel responsible for the breakdown in the relationship, questioning their actions, decisions, and mistakes. The parent who feels guilty may replay every interaction with their child, wondering if they said something wrong, made a poor choice, or failed to meet their

child's emotional needs. This type of self-blame can be paralyzing, preventing parents from seeing the bigger picture and hindering their ability to move forward.

3. **Shame**: Shame is another emotion that often accompanies estrangement. Parents may feel ashamed that their child has chosen to cut them off, interpreting the estrangement as a reflection of their inadequacy as a parent. This feeling of shame is particularly insidious because it strikes at the core of the parent's identity. In many cases, parents define themselves through their role as a caregiver, protector, and nurturer, so when that role is rejected, it can feel like a personal failure. Shame also tends to isolate parents, making it difficult for them to open up about their feelings or seek support, further deepening the emotional wound.

4. **Anger**: Anger often arises in response to the sense of injustice that parents feel. They may feel that they've been wronged by their child, that their love and efforts have been taken for granted, or that the estrangement was unnecessary. This anger can manifest as resentment toward the child, but it can also be directed inwardly, as parents wonder if they could have done more to prevent the estrangement. Anger can feel like a powerful emotion that gives parents the strength to confront their feelings, but if left unchecked, it can become destructive and prevent emotional healing.

5. **Sadness and Loneliness**: Sadness is perhaps the most persistent emotion in the emotional rollercoaster of estrangement. Parents may mourn the loss of the relationship, the memories, and the hope for the future that was once tied to their child. The sadness can be all-encompassing, leading to feelings of isolation and despair. Parents may feel as though they are alone in their grief, as estrangement is a difficult subject to discuss with others who may not understand the pain. This loneliness can deepen the sense of loss, creating a cycle of sadness that seems impossible to break.

The emotional terrain of estranged parents is complex and constantly shifting. It is not uncommon for parents to experience multiple emotions at once, and those emotions may fluctuate from day to day or even from moment to moment. One minute, they may feel a fleeting sense of hope that reconciliation is possible; the next, they may feel overwhelmed by sadness and hopelessness. These emotions can feel isolating and consuming, but they are a normal part of the grieving process.

Why Guilt and Shame Often Sabotage Healing

Among the many emotions that estranged parents experience, guilt and shame can be the most difficult to overcome. These emotions are often self-perpetuating and can prevent parents from moving toward healing.

1. **The Paralyzing Effect of Guilt**: Guilt is a powerful emotion that can keep parents stuck in a cycle of self-blame. It can cause them to constantly ruminate on the past, replaying every moment

of their relationship with their child in an attempt to pinpoint where they went wrong. This cycle of guilt often prevents parents from seeing the reality of the situation—they may convince themselves that they are solely responsible for the estrangement, even if the child's actions were also a factor. This internalized guilt can lead to feelings of helplessness and despair, making it harder for parents to take constructive steps toward healing.

When guilt becomes overwhelming, it can lead to a sense of hopelessness. Parents may feel as though they have already failed, and that no amount of effort will ever repair the relationship. This mindset can prevent them from seeking support or taking positive steps toward healing. The belief that they are solely to blame can trap parents in a negative emotional state, making it difficult to break free.

2. **The Toxicity of Shame**: Shame is often described as the feeling that there is something inherently wrong with oneself. Unlike guilt, which focuses on specific actions or behaviors, shame attacks the core of a person's identity. Parents who feel ashamed of the estrangement may internalize the belief that they are bad parents, unworthy of their child's love and respect. This belief can be incredibly isolating and self-destructive, making it difficult for parents to reach out for help or support.

Shame also prevents parents from experiencing the full range of their emotions. Instead of grieving in a healthy way, parents may suppress their feelings out of fear that they will be judged for their emotions. Shame may cause parents to withdraw from social situations or avoid talking about their pain, further deepening their isolation. The emotional wound created by shame is often hidden, making it all the more difficult to heal.

Additionally, shame can lead to self-sabotage. Parents may believe that they don't deserve happiness or peace, which can prevent them from pursuing healing strategies or seeking reconciliation with their child. This belief can perpetuate a cycle of emotional suffering, making it harder for parents to move forward and find peace.

Journaling, Therapy, and Safe Ways to Process Deep Emotional Pain

While guilt and shame can be incredibly difficult to overcome, it is possible to heal and process these emotions in healthy ways. One of the most effective methods for working through deep emotional pain is to allow oneself the space to feel and express emotions. This can be done through journaling, therapy, and other safe outlets for processing pain.

1. **Journaling**: Journaling is a powerful tool for estranged parents to express their emotions in a safe, private space. Writing about feelings of guilt, shame, anger, and sadness can help parents process these emotions and begin to release them. Journaling allows parents to reflect on their experiences, gain insight into their emotional state, and work through unresolved feelings without the fear of judgment.

When journaling, it is important for parents to allow themselves to write freely, without censoring their thoughts or emotions. The act of putting emotions onto paper can be cathartic, offering a sense of release and validation. Journaling can also serve as a way to track emotional progress over time, allowing parents to reflect on their healing journey and the steps they have taken toward emotional recovery.

2. **Therapy**: Therapy is an invaluable tool for estranged parents who are struggling with deep emotional pain. A therapist can provide a safe, non-judgmental space for parents to explore their feelings, gain perspective, and work through unresolved emotional issues. Therapy can help parents understand the root causes of their guilt and shame, and offer strategies for reframing negative thought patterns.

   For parents dealing with estrangement, therapy can also provide a space to explore family dynamics and uncover the underlying issues that may have contributed to the estrangement. Working with a therapist can help parents gain clarity, develop healthier coping strategies, and start the healing process.

3. **Safe Emotional Outlets**: In addition to journaling and therapy, there are other safe ways for estranged parents to process their emotions. These may include engaging in creative activities like art or music, practicing mindfulness or meditation, or participating in support groups for parents dealing with estrangement. The key is to find an outlet that allows for self-

expression and emotional release, while also promoting healing and self-compassion.

Conclusion

The emotional rollercoaster of estrangement is one of the most challenging and isolating experiences a parent can go through. From guilt and shame to anger and sadness, the emotional terrain is complicated and constantly shifting. Parents who experience estrangement often feel overwhelmed by the depth of their emotions, which can make it difficult to heal.

However, it is possible to begin the healing process by acknowledging and addressing the emotions that arise during estrangement. Guilt and shame, while powerful, do not have to define the parent's journey. By engaging in safe, healthy ways to process deep emotional pain—through journaling, therapy, and other emotional outlets—parents can begin to move through their grief and find a path forward. The journey may be long, but it is possible to heal, regain hope, and eventually find peace.

Chapter 5

Rewriting the Story – Breaking the Loop of Blame and Self-Doubt

Introduction

When a parent faces estrangement, the emotional narrative that unfolds can be filled with self-doubt, blame, and a sense of failure. The stories parents tell themselves about the breakdown of their relationships often become powerful forces in their emotional lives. These stories, rooted in grief and confusion, tend to focus on guilt and perceived mistakes. The mind runs in endless loops, replaying moments of conflict, words left unsaid, and decisions that now seem wrong. Over time, these narratives shape a parent's perception of themselves, their role, and their ability to ever rebuild the relationship.

However, one of the most important steps toward healing is rewriting this story. By breaking free from the cycle of blame and self-doubt, parents can transform the way they view their estrangement and, more importantly, the way they view themselves. In this chapter, we will explore the concept of narrative grief—how the stories we tell ourselves shape our emotions—and how parents can reframe their role in the relationship. Shifting from a mindset of failure to one of understanding and compassion is a pivotal step in breaking the emotional loop that keeps parents stuck in grief. Through reframing, parents can begin to see themselves not as failures but as individuals who were doing the best they could, navigating an incredibly complex and emotionally charged situation.

Understanding Narrative Grief and Emotional Storytelling

Grief is not just a series of emotional responses—it is also a process of storytelling. When we experience a loss, we tend to create narratives around that loss in order to make sense of it. This is especially true in the case of estrangement, where the loss is not final but ongoing. The stories we tell ourselves about the breakdown of the relationship can have a profound impact on how we experience and process the pain.

1. **The Power of the Story**: The narratives we construct during times of grief are not simply reflections of reality—they actively shape our reality. When parents experience estrangement, they often tell themselves a story in which they are to blame. This story might go something like, "I wasn't a good parent," or "I failed my child." These stories are grounded in feelings of guilt, shame, and a deep sense of inadequacy. Over time, this narrative becomes internalized, and parents begin to see themselves only through the lens of their perceived failure. They may feel trapped in this self-critical story, unable to move beyond it.

   This narrative grief, which focuses on self-blame, becomes a barrier to emotional healing. The more parents replay the story of their failure, the more they reinforce feelings of helplessness and hopelessness. These repeated thoughts fuel negative emotions and prevent parents from seeing the complexity of the estrangement or the possibility of resolution.

2. **The Role of Emotional Storytelling**: Emotional storytelling involves the way we frame our experiences and the emotions that accompany them. This storytelling shapes how we view ourselves and our relationships with others. When dealing with estrangement, the emotional story often focuses on perceived wrongdoings, missed opportunities, and unheeded warnings. The emotional pain is often locked in these stories, repeating endlessly and creating a sense of stuckness.

   Parents must become aware of the emotional stories they are telling themselves and recognize that these narratives are not static truths—they are dynamic and can be rewritten. The process of reframing involves challenging the old story, questioning its validity, and creating a new, more compassionate narrative that allows for healing and growth.

Reframing Your Parental Role in a Changed Relationship

A crucial step in healing from estrangement is the act of reframing one's role as a parent. Estrangement alters the parent-child relationship in ways that can feel like a complete loss, but it does not erase the fact that the parent has invested love, care, and effort into the relationship. The parent's role may no longer fit the idealized version of what they had hoped for, but that does not mean the parent has failed.

1. **Letting Go of the Idealized Role**: Parents often enter their roles with certain expectations—expectations that may not align with the reality of adult relationships. They may expect that they will always be needed, that their children will turn to them for guidance, and that their relationships will evolve into a mutually fulfilling adult dynamic. When estrangement occurs, these expectations are shattered, and the parent may feel as if their role has been invalidated.

   However, reframing involves letting go of the idealized role and accepting that relationships evolve. The parent may no longer play the role of the all-knowing, all-caring figure, but they can still be a source of support, understanding, and love—on their child's terms. Reframing doesn't mean abandoning the relationship, but rather shifting the parent's understanding of their role within it. It involves recognizing that, at any given moment, both parent and child are doing the best they can with the tools they have.

2. **Embracing the Complexity of the Parent-Child Relationship**: One of the hardest things for parents to accept in the face of estrangement is that relationships are inherently complex. A parent's love for their child doesn't always guarantee that the relationship will be smooth, harmonious, or free of conflict. Parents may have made mistakes, but they also made sacrifices and tried their best in an often difficult and unpredictable situation.

Reframing the parent-child relationship means acknowledging this complexity. It involves understanding that both parties bring their own experiences, emotions, and histories to the table. While estrangement may have been triggered by specific actions or events, it is likely that many factors have contributed to the breakdown—factors that go beyond the actions of just one person. Parents must shift from viewing the relationship in black-and-white terms (either a success or a failure) to seeing it as a nuanced, evolving connection that is shaped by both their actions and those of their child.

From "I Failed" to "We Were All Doing the Best We Could"

The shift from a mindset of failure to one of mutual understanding is perhaps the most important reframing step in the healing process. When parents see themselves as having "failed," they become stuck in a cycle of shame and guilt, unable to move forward. However, when they recognize that both they and their child were doing the best they could in difficult circumstances, they begin to free themselves from the self-blame that has kept them in emotional captivity.

1. **The Role of Compassionate Self-Talk**: One of the most powerful tools for reframing the narrative is compassionate self-talk. This involves speaking to oneself with kindness, understanding, and empathy—just as a parent would speak to a child who is struggling. Parents who are caught in a cycle of guilt and self-blame must learn to replace their negative self-talk with

more compassionate and realistic thoughts. Instead of saying, "I failed my child," they can reframe this as, "I did the best I could with the knowledge and resources I had at the time."

Compassionate self-talk helps parents move away from a punitive, self-critical mindset toward a more understanding and forgiving one. This shift is essential for healing, as it allows parents to step out of the emotional trap of guilt and shame and begin to see themselves with greater empathy.

2. **Recognizing the Limits of Control**: One of the hardest lessons for parents to accept is that they cannot control everything— especially the behavior and decisions of their adult children. While parents may have influence over their children's upbringing, they do not have the power to control the course of their adult children's lives or the choices they make in adulthood. Understanding this lack of control can be liberating. Parents can stop carrying the weight of responsibility for their child's decisions and instead focus on their own growth and healing.

Reframing the relationship means acknowledging that both parent and child are autonomous individuals who must navigate life in their own ways. While parents can still offer love and support, they must also accept that their child's path may diverge from their own hopes and expectations.

3. **Shifting from Failure to Growth**: Instead of viewing the estrangement as a failure, parents can reframe it as an opportunity for growth. Both parents and children are constantly evolving.

Estrangement, while painful, may ultimately lead to personal transformation for both parties. For parents, this might mean deepening their self-awareness, confronting unresolved emotional issues, and developing new ways of relating to others. For children, estrangement can be an opportunity to establish boundaries, assert independence, or work through their own personal struggles.

By shifting from a narrative of failure to one of growth, parents can begin to see estrangement not as the end of their relationship with their child, but as part of a larger, ongoing process of emotional development. This reframing allows for hope to remain alive—even if reconciliation seems distant.

Conclusion

Rewriting the emotional story of estrangement is a critical step in healing. Parents who have experienced estrangement often become trapped in a cycle of blame, guilt, and self-doubt, unable to see beyond their perceived failures. However, by understanding the power of narrative grief and emotional storytelling, parents can begin to rewrite their own stories. Reframing their role in the relationship, letting go of idealized expectations, and shifting from a mindset of failure to one of mutual understanding and compassion are essential steps in the process.

The journey of estrangement is difficult, and there are no easy answers. However, by rewriting the emotional narrative—focusing on the complexities of the relationship and recognizing that both parent and child were doing the best they could—parents can begin to heal, rebuild their sense of self-worth, and open the door to future possibilities. The process of reframing the story is not about erasing the pain but about transforming it, allowing parents to see themselves with greater compassion and understanding as they move forward on their healing journey.

Chapter 6

Letting Go Without Giving Up – The Art of Hopeful Surrender

Introduction

One of the most challenging aspects of estrangement is learning to navigate the delicate balance between holding on and letting go. Parents often find themselves in an emotional tug-of-war—desperate to fix the relationship, fearful of losing it entirely, and unsure of how to proceed when their child has distanced themselves. The instinct to cling, to try to control or force reconciliation, is natural. But the act of holding on too tightly can sometimes create more harm than good, both for the parent and for the relationship itself.

Letting go does not mean giving up love. It does not mean abandoning hope. Instead, letting go is a profound act of emotional wisdom, a decision to release control over things that are beyond one's power while continuing to hold space for love, healing, and the possibility of future connection. In this chapter, we will explore what it means to let go without giving up on the relationship. We will discuss the importance of healthy detachment—learning to create boundaries that protect emotional well-being without closing off love—and how to live with open hands, embracing the uncertainty of the estrangement while fostering personal growth and resilience.

What It Means to Let Go of Control Without Letting Go of Love

The notion of "letting go" often evokes images of giving up, of abandoning hope or the relationship itself. For parents going through estrangement, this idea can feel like a threat—a suggestion that they must stop loving their child, stop hoping for reconciliation, or even stop caring altogether. However, letting go in the context of estrangement is not about abandoning love or giving up on the possibility of healing. It is about releasing the illusion of control and allowing space for the relationship to evolve in its own time, without forcing outcomes.

1. **The Illusion of Control**: One of the hardest truths to accept in estrangement is that, as parents, we cannot control the actions or feelings of our children. Despite our best efforts, we cannot dictate their decisions, their perceptions of us, or the future of our relationship. Estranged parents often grapple with this lack of control, believing that if they just say the right thing, make the right gesture, or fix whatever went wrong, they can restore the relationship. This drive to control is fueled by the desire for certainty and resolution—a longing for the painful uncertainty of estrangement to end.

   However, trying to control the outcome of the estrangement can create more harm than good. It may lead to increased feelings of frustration, resentment, and helplessness. The truth is, control is an illusion in these situations. We cannot force another person to reconcile or to change their perspective. In order to move toward healing, parents must learn to let go of their need to control and accept that the future of the relationship may unfold in ways they cannot predict.

2. **Letting Go of Control, Not Love**: Letting go of control is not the same as giving up on the relationship. In fact, it is often an act of love in and of itself. It is about understanding that love does not require constant intervention or manipulation to thrive. Love is patient, and it allows for space, growth, and the freedom to make mistakes. Parents can love their children deeply without trying to control every aspect of the relationship. By letting go of the need for control, parents make room for their children to heal, grow, and potentially return when they are ready.

   Love, in this context, becomes unconditional—not based on the child's actions, but rather on the parent's ability to accept the estrangement with grace. Parents can love their child by respecting their autonomy, allowing them to make their own decisions, and trusting that, in time, the relationship may be restored. This kind of love is free from expectations and the pressure of immediate resolution. It allows parents to maintain hope without suffocating the relationship with demands.

Healthy Detachment: Not Coldness, But Boundaries with Grace

While letting go of control is essential, it is equally important to maintain healthy emotional boundaries. Healthy detachment allows parents to protect their emotional well-being while continuing to hold space for their child. This is not about coldness or indifference; rather, it is about establishing boundaries that honor both the parent's and the child's needs.

1. **Understanding Healthy Detachment**: Healthy detachment means being able to separate your own emotional well-being from the actions and decisions of your child. It is the ability to love deeply without becoming enmeshed in the other person's emotional state. For estranged parents, this means accepting that their child's decision to cut off communication is not a reflection of their worth as a person or a parent. Healthy detachment is about recognizing that, while you may feel pain, anger, or sadness over the estrangement, you are not responsible for carrying that burden indefinitely.

   Detachment is not about distancing oneself from love; it is about creating emotional space that allows both the parent and the child to breathe. It allows parents to honor their child's autonomy while still holding a place for them in their hearts. It is the recognition that the child's journey and healing process may be different from the parent's, and that each individual must move at their own pace.

2. **Boundaries with Grace**: The key to healthy detachment is establishing boundaries that protect your emotional health while allowing for the possibility of future connection. Boundaries with grace are those that are rooted in self-respect and compassion,

rather than fear or resentment. They are not meant to punish or control, but to create a space where both parties can heal.

For parents, this might mean stepping back from the relationship to give their child the space they need, while still expressing love and openness. This may look like refraining from repeatedly reaching out, sending letters, or trying to fix the relationship when the child is not ready to engage. It is about understanding that, while the parent's love and care remain, their child's autonomy must be respected.

Healthy detachment also means being mindful of how much emotional energy you invest in the estrangement. Constantly obsessing over what went wrong or replaying every interaction can be emotionally draining. Setting boundaries around your thoughts and emotions—by taking breaks from ruminating on the estrangement and focusing on your own self-care—can help preserve your mental and emotional well-being.

3. **Practicing Compassionate Boundaries**: Setting boundaries with grace is also about practicing self-compassion. It requires parents to acknowledge their pain without allowing it to define them. Parents must recognize that they, too, deserve emotional space to heal. By establishing these boundaries, parents model emotional maturity, showing their children that it is possible to love with respect and to detach with kindness. Compassionate boundaries are a way of preserving love without enabling unhealthy dynamics or sacrificing one's own peace of mind.

How to Live with Open Hands Instead of Clinging Fists

The image of open hands versus clinging fists captures the essence of letting go without giving up. A clenched fist represents control, grasping, and resistance—an unwillingness to release what we desire. On the other hand, open hands symbolize surrender, acceptance, and the willingness to receive what comes, even if it is uncertain or painful. Living with open hands is about embracing the present moment, acknowledging the limits of control, and accepting the possibility of change without attachment to outcomes.

1. **The Power of Surrender**: Surrender does not mean giving up hope; it means letting go of the need to control every aspect of the situation. It means trusting that, although the relationship is painful and uncertain, the future may still hold possibilities. Surrender is about releasing the attachment to specific outcomes and allowing life to unfold as it will. It is the courage to face the uncertainty of estrangement without constantly trying to "fix" it, while remaining open to the possibility of healing and connection in the future.

   For estranged parents, surrendering is an act of deep trust. It is about trusting that they have done their best, and that even if reconciliation does not happen immediately, there is still hope. It is trusting that the relationship can evolve, perhaps in ways that are beyond their current understanding. Surrender allows parents to release their grip on the situation while still holding a place of love in their hearts.

2. **The Freedom of Open Hands**: Living with open hands means letting go of the emotional burden that comes from clinging to the past or obsessing over the future. When parents cling to the idea of what their relationship with their child should look like, they remain trapped in a cycle of longing and disappointment. By living with open hands, parents can embrace the present moment, focusing on their own emotional healing and personal growth.

   This approach also allows parents to be open to other relationships—whether with other family members, friends, or even themselves. When parents live with open hands, they create space for love and healing to flow freely, without feeling weighed down by the pain of estrangement. It allows them to reclaim their sense of agency and to invest in their own emotional well-being, which, in turn, enables them to approach the estranged relationship from a place of strength, not desperation.

3. **Living in the Present, Not the Past**: One of the most powerful ways to live with open hands is to focus on the present rather than being consumed by the past. Parents who are fixated on what went wrong or who are constantly trying to predict the future of the relationship can become trapped in a cycle of emotional turmoil. By living in the present, parents can focus on the things they can control—such as their own healing, their own emotional well-being, and their capacity for love. This mindset

shift allows them to embrace the uncertainty of estrangement with grace, knowing that the future is always subject to change.

Conclusion

Letting go is one of the most difficult, yet transformative, aspects of navigating estrangement. It requires parents to release the need for control while still holding love and hope in their hearts. Healthy detachment, boundaries with grace, and living with open hands allow parents to navigate the uncertainty of estrangement with emotional resilience and personal growth.

Letting go does not mean giving up. It means accepting that, while you cannot control the course of the relationship, you can control how you respond. It is an act of trust—trust in yourself, in your child's journey, and in the possibility of reconciliation in the future. Through the art of hopeful surrender, parents can embrace the present moment, free themselves from the emotional burden of clinging to the past, and remain open to the future, whatever it may hold. In doing so, they allow both themselves and their children the space to heal and grow, while keeping love alive in their hearts.

Chapter 7

Messages Left Unsent – When Communication Breaks Down

Introduction

One of the hardest parts of estrangement is the silence. The moments when words are left unspoken, when messages go unsent, and when the phone remains unanswered. Silence often becomes the loudest voice in these situations. For estranged parents, the impulse to communicate—to reach out, explain, apologize, or repair the relationship—can feel almost overwhelming. Yet, at the same time, there is a deep, underlying fear of doing the wrong thing. What if reaching out causes more harm? What if your child is not ready, or worse, doesn't want to hear from you?

In this chapter, we will explore the delicate dynamics of communication during estrangement. Should you write a letter, or should you let silence speak for itself? We'll examine the temptation to "explain yourself" and why sometimes, respecting space can be the most loving thing to do. Additionally, we'll offer practical scripts and tools for non-invasive, open-hearted outreach that respects boundaries while keeping the door to communication open. The goal here is to navigate the tension between the desire to reach out and the necessity of respecting your child's space—without letting fear or frustration drive your actions.

Should You Write a Letter? When Silence Says More

One of the most common thoughts that crosses a parent's mind when estranged from their child is, "Should I write a letter?" Writing a letter is often seen as a way to bridge the gap between the estranged parent and child. It provides an opportunity to express thoughts, apologies, and hopes for reconciliation without the immediacy of a conversation. But while writing a letter can feel cathartic for the parent, it's important to carefully consider the timing, tone, and intent behind this gesture.

1. **The Purpose of the Letter**: Before deciding to write, it is important to reflect on why you want to write the letter in the first place. Is it to explain yourself, to express your feelings, or to make amends? Are you hoping the letter will initiate reconciliation, or is it simply an attempt to release some of your own emotional burden? The answer to these questions will shape the content and tone of the letter.

    o **If the goal is to explain yourself**: There is a temptation to justify your actions, provide context, or clarify misunderstandings. However, it's important to remember that the child may not be open to hearing explanations at this time. Often, the estranged child is not seeking clarification; they are seeking space, or they may have already made sense of the situation in their own way. Over-explaining can sometimes feel defensive, and it may unintentionally shift the focus from their feelings to your own. In these cases, it might be better to wait until there is more openness in the relationship before sending a letter.

○ **If the goal is to express your feelings**: If you're writing the letter to express your emotions—such as sorrow, regret, or love—it's important to write with compassion and vulnerability. Let the letter reflect your true feelings, without pressure to fix anything or seek an immediate resolution. Focus on expressing love, understanding, and openness, rather than on trying to change the situation.

2. **When Silence Says More**: Sometimes, the most respectful form of communication is silence. If your child has asked for space, or if communication has been cut off, sending a letter may not be the right choice. Silence, in these cases, is a powerful and respectful gesture that communicates your understanding of their need for time and distance. It allows your child the space to process their emotions without feeling pressured.

The silence between you may feel unbearable, but it can also be a reflection of respect for your child's boundaries. Instead of filling that silence with your own need to reach out, it may be more beneficial to embrace it. Silence can also offer a message of unconditional love—by holding space without demanding a response, you signal to your child that you love them without expectation or condition.

3. **The Timing of the Letter**: Even if a letter feels like the right choice, timing is crucial. It's important to consider whether your child is in a place where they are ready to hear from you. A letter sent too soon—while emotions are still raw—may be met with rejection or further distance. However, over time, as both parties have time to process their emotions, a letter may be the right form of outreach. A letter allows your child to engage with your words when they are ready, at their own pace.

Navigating the Temptation to "Explain Yourself" vs. Respecting Space

When estrangement occurs, parents often feel a deep urge to explain their side of the story. The impulse to "explain yourself" is natural, especially when you feel misunderstood or when you believe that your actions have been misinterpreted. However, the act of explaining often conflicts with the need to respect space—one of the most important boundaries in the estrangement process.

1. **The Need to Be Heard**: When parents are estranged, they often feel that they have not had a chance to fully express themselves. This lack of communication can lead to frustration, resentment, and an overwhelming desire to justify their actions. However, explaining yourself can sometimes hinder rather than help the healing process. Often, the child who has chosen estrangement is not in a place where they are ready or willing to listen to explanations. They may feel that their needs have been ignored

or dismissed for so long that the act of explaining may come across as self-serving or defensive.

Instead of seeking immediate validation or an opportunity to defend yourself, it may be more beneficial to focus on expressing your feelings without trying to correct or fix the past. Parents may need to sit with the discomfort of being misunderstood, acknowledging that their child's feelings are valid, even if they are based on a perception that doesn't fully align with their own experience.

2. **Respecting Space vs. The Urge to Fix**: One of the most difficult aspects of estrangement is resisting the temptation to "fix" the situation. Parents often feel that by explaining themselves or offering an apology, they can right the wrongs of the past and restore the relationship. However, forcing communication before the child is ready can undermine their sense of autonomy and further damage the relationship.

It's important to understand that respecting space doesn't mean abandoning your child—it means giving them the room they need to process their emotions, come to terms with their own feelings, and make decisions in their own time. By refraining from overwhelming your child with communication or emotional pleas, you signal that you are respecting their autonomy and emotional needs.

Sometimes, the best way to show love is not through words, but through actions. Giving your child space to heal allows them the opportunity to come back when they are ready, free from the pressure to reconcile on anyone else's terms.

Scripts and Tools for Non-Invasive, Open-Hearted Outreach

While respecting space is essential, there may still be moments when parents feel ready to reach out in a gentle, non-invasive way. The key to successful outreach is to focus on open-hearted, non-demanding communication that invites connection without pushing for a response. Below are some scripts and tools for parents who wish to reach out, with the understanding that they must be prepared for a range of reactions— or no reaction at all.

1. **A Simple Message of Love and Support**: Sometimes, a brief message of love and support is enough to show that you care without demanding a response. This message should be simple, heartfelt, and free from any expectations. For example:

   ○ **Script**: "I just wanted to let you know that I love you, and I'm thinking of you. I understand that you may need space, and I respect that. Whenever you're ready, I'm here. Take care."

   This message communicates love and respect for the child's autonomy while keeping the door to communication open. It doesn't pressure the child for a response, nor does it offer an explanation for past actions.

2. **An Apology without Demands**: If the estrangement is rooted in misunderstandings or past mistakes, an apology may be necessary. However, it's crucial that the apology is free from expectations or demands for reconciliation. The goal is to take ownership of one's actions, without using the apology as a way to fix the relationship.

   ○ **Script**: "I'm truly sorry for the hurt I caused. I understand if you're angry or upset, and I don't want to pressure you. I just want you to know that I deeply regret the pain I've caused, and I'm here when you're ready to talk."

This apology acknowledges the child's feelings, offers responsibility without justification, and leaves the door open for future communication.

3. **Expressing Boundaries with Love**: Sometimes, estranged parents may want to express their own needs or boundaries without alienating their child further. A message that shares these needs can still be loving and respectful, while making it clear that healing requires both parties to have their boundaries respected.

   ○ **Script**: "I understand that we may be in different places right now, and I respect your need for space. I just want to let you know that I am committed to my own healing and will continue to respect your boundaries. I'm here when you're ready to reconnect."

This message asserts the parent's own need for healing and acknowledges that the estranged relationship will take time and mutual effort to repair.

4. **Sending a Letter with No Expectations**: If a letter feels like the right choice, it should be written without any expectations for a response. The tone should be calm, compassionate, and focused on expressing love and understanding.

    o **Script**: "I have been thinking a lot about our relationship, and I just wanted to reach out. I'm not expecting anything from you, but I want you to know that I love you deeply, and I hope that in time we can find a way to reconnect. Until then, I will respect your space and continue to hold you in my heart."

    This letter communicates deep affection and understanding, while making it clear that the parent is not demanding anything from the child, just offering unconditional love.

Conclusion

Communication during estrangement is one of the most delicate aspects of the journey. The temptation to reach out and explain oneself is natural, but it is important to navigate this desire with sensitivity, respecting both your child's space and their emotional needs. Whether through writing a letter, sending a simple message, or maintaining silence, the key is to approach communication with an open heart and a willingness to respect boundaries. Non-invasive outreach—focused on love, understanding, and patience—can open the door to future reconciliation, without pressuring your child or further complicating the estrangement.

Estrangement is a painful journey, but through thoughtful and compassionate communication, estranged parents can foster the conditions for healing.

Chapter 8

Navigating Holidays, Birthdays, and Family Gatherings

Introduction

Holidays, birthdays, and family gatherings are meant to be times of joy and connection. Yet, for estranged parents, these events can become overwhelming reminders of the emotional distance between themselves and their children. These occasions—charged with tradition, family expectations, and emotional significance—can trigger deep grief flare-ups, feelings of loss, and painful memories. For many, the absence of a child at these gatherings is a sharp reminder of the estrangement, and the celebrations that once brought comfort and unity can now feel like burdens to bear.

In this chapter, we will explore how estranged parents can navigate major life events like holidays, birthdays, and family gatherings while managing the grief and emotional turbulence that often arise. We will discuss how to handle grief flare-ups during these events, the importance of creating new rituals and traditions that honor healing, and how to deal with other family members who may take sides or avoid the topic altogether. The goal is to empower estranged parents to approach these emotional minefields with strength, compassion, and a renewed sense of hope, allowing them to reclaim peace and healing during times that might otherwise feel impossible to face.

How to Handle Grief Flare-Ups During Major Events

Grief often flares up unexpectedly, especially during major events that carry emotional weight. Birthdays, holidays, and family gatherings serve as poignant reminders of what has been lost—the relationships, the shared memories, and the hopes for the future. For estranged parents, these events can trigger intense waves of sorrow, anger, guilt, or even resentment. Understanding how to manage grief flare-ups in these moments is essential for maintaining emotional well-being.

1. **Anticipating the Emotional Impact**: One of the first steps in handling grief during major events is to acknowledge the emotional impact that these occasions will likely have. If the estrangement is still fresh, it's important to prepare yourself for the inevitable sadness and potential triggers that may arise. This might mean acknowledging that the absence of your child will hurt, and that it's okay to feel that pain. Instead of trying to push those feelings aside, give yourself permission to experience them. Grief is not linear, and it may resurface during these events in ways you did not expect.

2. **Setting Realistic Expectations**: Holidays and family gatherings often come with an unspoken pressure to be happy or put on a brave face. However, setting realistic expectations for yourself is crucial. It's okay to acknowledge that you may not be able to fully embrace the festive spirit this year. You may need to create space

for both grief and celebration—allowing yourself to mourn while also finding moments of joy. By accepting that your experience of the event may differ from previous years, you can ease the pressure to "perform" for others and focus on honoring your emotional needs.

3. **Finding Safe Ways to Express Emotions**: During family gatherings, it's often difficult to fully express the depth of your grief, especially if others don't understand or acknowledge the estrangement. One way to manage grief flare-ups is by finding safe, private outlets for your emotions. This might include taking a quiet walk outside to cry, journaling your feelings before or after the event, or even finding a trusted friend or therapist to talk to. Creating space to express your emotions in a healthy way can prevent them from becoming overwhelming during the event itself.

4. **Embracing the Power of "Small Wins"**: While it may be tempting to focus on the absence of your child, it can be helpful to shift your attention to the small wins—those moments of connection or peace that may arise during the gathering. Whether it's sharing a laugh with a family member, enjoying a meal, or simply sitting in quiet reflection, these small moments can help anchor you and remind you that, even in the midst of pain, healing is possible.

5. **Having a Plan for Triggering Moments**: There will likely be moments during family gatherings when the grief becomes

overwhelming. Perhaps there will be a mention of your child, an empty chair, or a photo that brings back memories. Having a plan for these triggering moments can help you manage your emotions. This plan might include having a quiet retreat space to collect yourself, using grounding techniques (like deep breathing or mindfulness), or simply acknowledging the emotion without judgment and allowing it to pass. The goal is not to suppress the grief, but to manage it in a way that is not destructive to your emotional well-being.

Creating New Rituals and Traditions That Honor Healing

For estranged parents, holding on to old traditions and rituals can sometimes deepen the pain of the estrangement. The customs and practices that once brought comfort—whether it's decorating the tree, exchanging gifts, or sharing a holiday meal—may now serve as reminders of what is missing. However, rather than clinging to what has been lost, creating new rituals and traditions can be a powerful way to honor healing, growth, and the evolving nature of family life.

1. **Letting Go of Outdated Traditions**: It can be difficult to let go of the traditions that were once integral to your family's celebrations. These traditions represent love, unity, and shared history. However, if these traditions now feel painful or emotionally charged due to estrangement, it might be time to let them go—at least for the time being. This doesn't mean abandoning family celebrations altogether; rather, it's about

recognizing that the old ways of doing things may no longer serve you or your emotional needs.

For example, if a particular family ritual brings up painful memories of your estranged child, consider skipping it or modifying it in a way that feels more supportive of your current emotional state. Letting go of these rituals can create space for healing and help you navigate the event with more peace.

2. **Creating New Traditions for Yourself**: One of the most empowering ways to move forward is to create new traditions that reflect your current reality—ones that honor your healing process and provide opportunities for growth. These new rituals can be simple and personal, such as lighting a candle in memory of the relationship, taking a moment of silence to reflect on the past year, or volunteering for a cause that resonates with you. These new traditions allow you to reclaim the power of the holiday or family event in a way that feels nurturing and healing, rather than painful.

For example, instead of focusing on the absence of your child, you could create a ritual of writing a letter or note to them each year. This act of acknowledgment allows you to express love, regret, and hope while also providing a space for healing. Alternatively, you might start a tradition of taking a solo retreat or spending time in nature during the holiday season, using this time to reconnect with yourself and reflect on your emotional journey.

3. **Involving Other Family Members in Healing**: If you are comfortable, consider involving other family members in the creation of new rituals. This could be a way to build bridges and heal together. For instance, instead of focusing on old family traditions, you could create new ones that reflect a sense of togetherness and healing. A simple tradition like sharing what you're grateful for or acknowledging each other's emotional journeys can strengthen the bonds within the family. By consciously creating new rituals that honor everyone's experiences, you can infuse the holiday with a sense of hope and connection, even in the face of estrangement.

4. **Flexibility and Openness**: It's important to approach new traditions with flexibility. What works one year might not work the next, and that's okay. The goal is not perfection or adherence to specific practices, but the intention to create an environment where healing and growth are prioritized. Be open to changing the tradition as you evolve, and allow yourself the grace to adapt as needed.

Dealing with Other Family Members Who "Take Sides" or Avoid the Topic

Estrangement can often lead to tension not only between the estranged parent and child but also within the larger family system. Other family members may struggle with the estrangement in different ways. Some may take sides, aligning themselves with one party or the other, while others may avoid the topic altogether, uncomfortable with the emotional complexity of the situation. For estranged parents, navigating these dynamics can be challenging, but it's important to approach these interactions with self-compassion and a clear sense of boundaries.

1. **Managing Family "Sides"**: When family members take sides, it can feel like a betrayal or an additional source of pain. It's important to acknowledge these feelings but not allow them to derail your healing. While you may feel hurt by the way other family members have reacted, remember that their responses are often rooted in their own discomfort or lack of understanding. It is not your responsibility to change their feelings or make them "pick a side."

   Instead of focusing on the family dynamic, try to focus on your own emotional needs. Set clear boundaries with family members who push you to take action or "fix" the situation. You are not obligated to justify your decisions or defend your actions to others. A respectful, non-confrontational way to address this might be: "I understand that this situation is difficult for everyone, but I need to focus on healing right now, and I ask for your understanding and respect for my emotional space."

2. **Handling Avoidance or Silence**: When other family members avoid the topic of estrangement, it can feel isolating. The silence around the issue can create tension, and you may feel like you're expected to pretend everything is fine. In these situations, it's important to respect your own emotional boundaries and decide when and how to bring up the topic, if at all. You have the right

to express your feelings, but you are not obligated to do so if it will cause unnecessary conflict or further emotional harm.

You may choose to simply acknowledge the estrangement in a quiet, dignified way, without going into detail. A brief, honest statement such as, "This is a really difficult time for me, and I appreciate your support" can let others know that you are open to acknowledging the situation without delving into it. This allows you to honor your own feelings without putting pressure on others to respond or take sides.

3. **Taking Care of Your Own Emotional Needs**: Above all, remember that you are the one navigating the emotional terrain of estrangement. While other family members may offer their opinions, it's important to prioritize your own emotional well-being. You are not responsible for how others handle the situation, and it's okay to set boundaries with family members who are unhelpful or emotionally draining. Focus on creating an environment where your healing is prioritized, whether that means limiting interactions with certain family members or choosing not to engage in conversations that feel emotionally taxing.

Conclusion

Holidays, birthdays, and family gatherings are deeply emotional milestones for estranged parents, often bringing grief flare-ups and complicated family dynamics to the forefront. While these events may trigger sadness and remind parents of what has been lost, they also offer an opportunity to create new rituals, honor personal healing, and maintain boundaries with grace. By approaching these gatherings with self-compassion, managing grief with patience, and setting clear emotional boundaries, estranged parents can navigate these occasions with strength and resilience.

The key to surviving these emotional events is not in pretending everything is okay, but in allowing yourself to feel what you need to feel, while also making space for healing. Whether it's through creating new traditions, respecting space, or dealing with family dynamics, the goal is to move through the event with dignity and hope, honoring your own journey of healing while leaving the door open for the possibility of reconnection in the future.

Chapter 9

Rebuilding a Life – Identity Beyond Parenthood

Introduction

When a parent experiences estrangement, it can feel as though their entire identity is unraveling. Parenthood has been such a significant part of their life, their identity, and their sense of purpose, and suddenly, when that bond is fractured, it can feel like a profound loss of self. Estranged parents often wrestle with feelings of inadequacy, shame, and confusion, especially as they navigate a world that continues to function as though everything is "normal" while they feel deeply wounded. Their role as parents, once central to their identity, is no longer what it was—and with it, they may feel as though they've lost their sense of who they are.

However, estrangement offers an opportunity to rediscover the wholeness that extends beyond the role of a parent. Rebuilding a life after estrangement is not about "filling the void" left by your child, but rather about reclaiming your own personhood, your passions, your purpose, and your connection to the world. In this chapter, we will explore how estranged parents can rebuild their lives by reconnecting with their identity beyond parenthood. We'll discuss how to reclaim your wholeness as a human being, find new meaning, build community, and explore passions and connections that bring fulfillment outside the parental role.

Reclaiming Your Wholeness as a Human Being

Estrangement often leaves parents questioning their worth and sense of self. If they've defined themselves primarily through their role as a parent, the loss of that relationship can feel like a loss of identity itself. However, one of the most crucial steps in rebuilding life after estrangement is recognizing that your identity is not solely tied to parenthood. You are a complete, multifaceted person with a unique history, interests, and potential—whether or not you are actively involved in the life of your child.

1. **Acknowledge the Loss, But Don't Let It Define You**: It is natural to grieve the relationship with your child and the role you no longer play in their life. However, it's equally important to understand that the estrangement does not define you as a person. Yes, your identity as a parent was important, but that identity was only one piece of the puzzle. You have lived a life full of experiences, and those experiences contribute to the richness of who you are. Take time to reflect on your strengths, the accomplishments you've achieved, and the qualities that make you unique.

2. **Rediscover Who You Are Without the Title of "Parent"**: This process can be a challenging but liberating journey of self-discovery. Who were you before you became a parent? What activities brought you joy or fulfillment before your focus was on

70

your children? Reconnecting with those parts of yourself that may have been sidelined during the intense focus on parenthood is vital. Perhaps it's a long-lost hobby, a creative pursuit, or a career ambition that you put on hold. Take time to rediscover what lights you up and brings you joy outside of your role as a parent.

3. **Begin by asking yourself questions like**:

   ○ What do I truly enjoy doing for myself?

   ○ What are my personal goals, independent of my children's needs?

   ○ How can I invest in my own growth and development moving forward?

4. **Let Go of Guilt Around Self-Care**: Many parents may feel guilty when they begin focusing on themselves, believing that their attention should always be directed toward their children. This guilt can hinder self-compassion and delay the process of healing. It's essential to let go of the idea that self-care is selfish. By reclaiming your personal identity and nurturing your well-being, you are not abandoning your child; you are simply allowing yourself to heal and grow. This self-compassion not only benefits you but also prepares you to offer healthier, more grounded support to your child if and when reconciliation occurs.

Finding Meaning, Community, and Purpose Outside the Parental Role

When estranged parents lose the connection with their child, they often feel a profound sense of purposelessness. The day-to-day routine of parenting, nurturing, and caregiving may have defined their sense of purpose for years. Without this role, life can feel empty or aimless. However, this is an opportunity to discover new sources of meaning and purpose that align with your current life circumstances.

1. **Finding New Purpose**: The loss of one purpose doesn't mean the end of your sense of purpose altogether. The question becomes: What do you want your life to represent now? You can find new purpose in areas that are deeply meaningful to you. It could be returning to an old passion, contributing to causes you care about, or dedicating your time to a new project or goal.

   For example, many estranged parents find purpose in volunteer work, whether it's helping others who are going through similar struggles, supporting community organizations, or contributing their skills in a way that aligns with their values. The key is to find something that sparks passion and provides a sense of contribution to the world, beyond the relationship with your child.

2. **Building a New Community**: Estrangement can feel isolating, especially if the breakdown in your relationship with your child has led to the dissolution of other family or social connections. However, this is an opportunity to build new relationships, both

with people who understand your experience and with those who offer fresh perspectives.

Consider seeking out support groups for parents of estranged children, or participating in activities and communities where you can meet new people with shared interests. Whether through hobbies, classes, spiritual gatherings, or local meet-ups, cultivating relationships with others who respect and value you can help fill the gap left by estrangement. Building a new sense of community can be a powerful way to rebuild your life and feel connected again.

3. **Exploring Spiritual Connection**: Many estranged parents turn to spirituality to find meaning and healing during this difficult time. Spiritual practices such as meditation, prayer, mindfulness, or attending religious services can offer a sense of peace, grounding, and connection to something larger than oneself. These practices can provide emotional relief, help manage grief, and encourage a sense of purpose that transcends the pain of estrangement.

Spirituality can also encourage a deeper sense of forgiveness— both toward yourself and, potentially, your child. It can be an avenue for personal transformation, allowing you to explore the broader lessons that this challenging experience may offer. Connecting with a supportive spiritual community can also help you find comfort and encouragement during this time of emotional rebuilding.

Exploring Passions, Friendships, and Spiritual Connection

As you begin to rebuild your life, it's essential to embrace your passions, deepen friendships, and explore your spiritual connection. Each of these areas contributes to your overall sense of well-being and can serve as a path toward healing.

1. **Rediscovering Passions**: Often, estranged parents have put their personal passions on hold in order to focus on their children's needs. Now is the time to rediscover those activities or interests that once brought joy and fulfillment. Whether it's painting, writing, gardening, dancing, or traveling, engaging in activities that ignite your creativity and bring you joy can provide an incredible sense of personal satisfaction. Rediscovering or cultivating new passions will help you reconnect with your true self and create a sense of vitality outside the context of parenthood.

2. **Strengthening Friendships**: Friendships are often neglected during the intense years of parenting, particularly when the focus is solely on the child. Rebuilding your life after estrangement involves reconnecting with old friends or making new ones who support and uplift you. Friendships offer emotional support, laughter, and companionship, which are essential for healing. Whether it's sharing a cup of coffee with a close friend or participating in social activities, friendships can be a source of nourishment for your soul.

3. **Fostering Meaningful Connections**: Beyond simply finding new friends, it's important to nurture relationships that offer emotional depth and mutual understanding. Seek out people who share your values and who appreciate you for who you are, not just as a parent. These connections can help you feel seen, validated, and supported as you rebuild your life. Meaningful relationships enrich your sense of self-worth and provide a foundation for healing.

4. **Spiritual Exploration**: Many people find solace in spirituality during difficult times. Whether through formal religious practices, personal meditation, or philosophical exploration, spiritual connection offers a sense of grounding, peace, and comfort. Spiritual practices can help you process the complex emotions of estrangement and guide you toward a place of acceptance, forgiveness, and peace. Through spiritual exploration, you can connect with a higher purpose and gain clarity on your journey toward healing.

Conclusion

Rebuilding your life after estrangement is a deeply personal and transformative journey. It is about reclaiming your wholeness, rediscovering your passions, and finding new meaning outside the role of a parent. Estranged parents often experience a profound loss of identity and purpose, but this is also an opportunity to reconnect with oneself, build new relationships, and find fulfillment in different areas of life.

As you move forward, remember that your identity is multifaceted. You are not just a parent, but a person with unique experiences, dreams, and aspirations. By embracing new passions, fostering meaningful connections, and exploring your spiritual life, you can rebuild a life that is rich with purpose and meaning. This journey may take time, but by focusing on self-compassion, growth, and healing, you can emerge stronger, wiser, and more whole than ever before.

Chapter 10

When Estrangement Ends – Reunions, Relapses, and Redefinitions

Introduction

The possibility of reconciliation after estrangement is one of the most complex and emotionally charged aspects of the journey. When estranged parents experience the return of their child—whether through a letter, a phone call, or an actual meeting—it can be a moment of profound relief, joy, and healing. However, it is also often fraught with uncertainty. What does reconciliation look like? How do you navigate the emotional intensity of reestablishing a connection? And, perhaps most importantly, how do you manage the potential for relapse into the estrangement cycle?

In this chapter, we will explore what parents can expect when reconciliation happens, the emotional pitfalls to avoid, and how to build trust in fragile reunions. We will also discuss the importance of accepting new boundaries and redefining the relationship—understanding that while reconciliation is a hopeful and healing process, it does not mean returning to the past or "fixing" everything that went wrong. Instead, reconciliation is about moving forward, creating a new dynamic, and finding a way to coexist that honors the growth and changes each person has undergone during the period of estrangement.

If Reconciliation Happens: What to Expect, What to Avoid

Reconciliation after estrangement is not a magical or immediate fix; it is a gradual, sometimes uncertain process that requires patience, understanding, and respect. It's important for parents to enter this process with realistic expectations and a willingness to embrace the ambiguity of this new phase in the relationship.

1. **Expecting Imperfection**: Reconciliation is a process, not an event. While the return of a child may feel like the resolution of the estrangement, it doesn't mean that everything will automatically be fixed. There will be bumps along the way, emotional triggers, and the need for deep conversations to unpack the past. The relationship that existed before estrangement may not be the same as the one that emerges after reconciliation, and that's okay. Expecting perfection or rushing toward "normalcy" can put unnecessary pressure on both parties and derail the healing process. It's important to accept that things may feel awkward, uncertain, or even uncomfortable at times.

   Example: After a period of estrangement, a parent might expect their child to quickly revert to the role they once had in their life. However, the child may have changed emotionally, psychologically, or spiritually during the estrangement. A parent should approach the reunion with patience, understanding that their child may need time to re-engage, and that the relationship will likely develop in new ways.

2. **Emotions May Be Overwhelming**: When estrangement ends, emotions often come flooding back. While the feeling of reunion may bring a sense of joy, it's not uncommon for other emotions—such as guilt, anger, or resentment—to arise as well. These emotions can be complicated, especially if there has been a long period of silence or hurt. Both the parent and the child may need to navigate these emotions carefully, respecting each other's feelings without rushing to "fix" them. Being mindful of emotional highs and lows, and allowing space for feelings to be expressed without judgment, is essential for the healing process.

3. **What to Avoid**: During the initial stages of reconciliation, it's crucial to avoid certain behaviors that could hinder the process. One of the biggest pitfalls is rushing to explain, justify, or apologize for everything that went wrong during the estrangement. While apologies and explanations may eventually be necessary, the first step is to simply listen, validate, and acknowledge the emotions of the other person. If a parent jumps too quickly into "fixing" things or explaining their actions, it can come across as defensive or dismissive of the child's feelings.

   Example: If a child expresses anger about the estrangement or the parent's actions, it's important for the parent to acknowledge their feelings and provide space for those emotions to be heard. Avoiding the temptation to immediately defend oneself or explain actions is key in allowing the child to process their own emotions and contribute to a genuine conversation.

4. **Keep Expectations Flexible**: While it's natural to feel hope when reconciliation begins, it's important to manage expectations. Both parent and child may have changed during the period of estrangement, and the reunion may not look exactly as either party had imagined. Expecting an immediate return to a previous dynamic—or even rushing the relationship to "catch up" with lost time—can set both parties up for disappointment. Instead, approach the reunion with an open mind and a willingness to build something new, recognizing that it will take time and effort for both sides to adjust.

Trust-Building in Fragile Reunions

Trust is one of the most fragile aspects of any relationship, and when estrangement has occurred, rebuilding that trust can be especially challenging. It's important to recognize that trust is something that must be earned, not demanded, and that it takes time, patience, and consistency to restore. Both parents and children must be willing to take small steps toward rebuilding trust without rushing the process.

1. **The Role of Vulnerability**: For trust to be rebuilt, both parties need to be open and vulnerable. This means being willing to express emotions honestly— without trying to hide behind walls or deflect pain. Parents should be prepared to hear difficult truths from their child, and children should be willing to acknowledge the hurt that may have been caused during the estrangement. Vulnerability creates the space for genuine connection and understanding.

Example: If a parent has to admit their mistakes in the estrangement, they may need to express regret for specific actions, and also be open to hearing their child's perspective. Similarly, the child may need to share their feelings of hurt and disappointment, knowing that their parent is willing to listen without judgment.

2. **Consistency and Patience**: Rebuilding trust requires consistent effort over time. Both the parent and child must commit to showing up for each other, proving that they can be reliable, caring, and understanding. Trust is not built on grand gestures; rather, it's built on small, everyday actions—showing up for each other, respecting boundaries, and acknowledging each other's emotional needs.

    Example: A parent might say, "I understand you need time before we can talk openly, and I respect that. I'm here when you're ready." This consistent approach to respecting boundaries, while still expressing love and patience, helps rebuild trust over time.

3. **Accepting Setbacks**: Trust-building is rarely a straight line. It's important to recognize that setbacks are a normal part of the process. Emotional triggers, past hurts, or old patterns of behavior may resurface during the reunion, causing moments of tension or conflict. Both parent and child need to approach these setbacks with patience and understanding, recognizing that these are opportunities for growth rather than reasons to give up.

Healing is not linear, and reconciliation will require time, setbacks, and efforts to repair the relationship after moments of difficulty.

Accepting New Boundaries Without Needing to "Go Back to How It Was"

One of the most difficult aspects of reconciliation is coming to terms with the fact that the relationship will never be the same as it was before the estrangement. Both parent and child have changed during the time apart, and these changes should be respected and acknowledged as part of the healing process. Understanding that the relationship must evolve and adapt to new circumstances, rather than simply trying to "return to how it was," is crucial for lasting reconciliation.

1. **The Need for New Boundaries**: With the return of communication or contact, it's important for both the parent and child to establish new boundaries that are respectful of each other's emotional needs. The boundaries that existed before the estrangement may no longer be appropriate, as both parties have likely changed in ways that require reevaluation of the relationship dynamics.

   Example: If a parent used to be very involved in their child's life decisions but their child has now become more independent, it may be necessary to adjust the parent's level of involvement. Similarly, a child may need to communicate how much contact they are comfortable with, whether it's frequency of phone calls or the types of conversations they're willing to have.

2. **Letting Go of the "Old" Relationship**: One of the most challenging aspects of reconciliation is accepting that the relationship must be redefined. The past is, in many ways, gone. This doesn't mean that the love or the bond has disappeared, but it does mean that the relationship must evolve to reflect the new realities of both people. Trying to resurrect the past—by forcing things to go back to "how it was"—can be damaging to the healing process.

   Example: A parent may long for the days when their child was young and they had more direct influence and control over their life. However, with adulthood comes a new relationship dynamic—one based more on mutual respect, independence, and understanding. Letting go of the idealized version of the past allows both parties to embrace the present and build a new foundation for their relationship moving forward.

3. **Building a Relationship on New Terms**: Reconciliation doesn't mean that everything is forgiven or that all past wounds are erased. Instead, it's about finding a new way to relate to each other, based on current realities and a shared desire to heal. This means being open to the changes that both parent and child have undergone during the estrangement and respecting each other's emotional journeys. It also means being flexible and open to the possibility that the relationship may look different but can still be meaningful and loving.

Example: If a parent and child have differing opinions or lifestyles, they may need to navigate those differences with respect. Instead of forcing the other person to change or adopting an "all-or-nothing" mentality, they can focus on the love and respect that still exists, while accepting their differences as part of the process of reconnection.

Conclusion

When estrangement ends and reconciliation begins, the journey toward rebuilding the relationship is just as complex and nuanced as the estrangement itself. It requires patience, vulnerability, and a willingness to redefine the relationship. Both parent and child must navigate the challenges of rebuilding trust, setting new boundaries, and accepting that the relationship may never return to the way it was—but can still be meaningful, loving, and fulfilling in new ways.

By approaching reconciliation with an open heart, realistic expectations, and a commitment to respect and healing, estranged parents and their children can rebuild their connection, not by resurrecting the past, but by creating a new, healthier relationship that honors both their growth and their shared history. The road to reconciliation may be long, but with empathy, understanding, and patience, the possibility of a stronger, more authentic bond is always within reach.

Chapter 11

Staying Connected to Love – Even Without Contact

Introduction

When estrangement happens, the desire to maintain a loving connection with your child often remains unwavering, even though physical or verbal contact may be limited or nonexistent. The heartbreaking reality is that love, though present, may not always have the outlet you once imagined. And yet, the power of unconditional love doesn't depend on proximity or communication. Love, when practiced from a distance, can take on a new form—quiet, steadfast, and ever-present—an expression of care and compassion that doesn't require reciprocity. In fact, the deepest love is often the one that expects nothing in return but continues to offer light, even in the darkness.

In this chapter, we will explore how estranged parents can continue to stay connected to love even without direct contact. We will discuss the practice of unconditional love from a distance, rituals and prayers that can offer comfort and a sense of connection, and the quiet, ongoing acts of care that affirm your commitment to your child's well-being, even when the relationship feels distant. We will also delve into the importance of loving with an open heart—without the expectation of immediate reconciliation, but with the belief that the door to love is always open.

Practicing Unconditional Love from a Distance

Unconditional love is often described as love that does not depend on the other person's actions or behaviors. It is a love that is given freely, regardless of circumstances, and it transcends any conditions or expectations. In the context of estrangement, unconditional love is an essential practice for parents who continue to love their children, even when communication has been severed. This kind of love is not about fixing the relationship, but about offering compassion and care from afar.

1. **Understanding Unconditional Love**: Unconditional love is not about accepting harmful behaviors or ignoring the need for boundaries. It is not a passive or blind love, but one that respects the autonomy of both the parent and the child. This type of love acknowledges the pain of estrangement, yet continues to exist in a space that does not demand change or reconciliation in order to be valid.

   Practicing unconditional love means loving your child in the fullest sense, even when they are not present or even when they may not feel ready to return that love. It is about giving from a place of inner strength, rather than from a place of need or expectation. Unconditional love allows parents to continue holding their child in their hearts, even as the relationship is being redefined.

2. **Letting Go of Expectations**: One of the hardest aspects of estrangement is the deep yearning for connection, the desire for things to go back to how they were. Unconditional love requires

that parents let go of these expectations, recognizing that their child may need space, may not be able to give love in return, or may never be ready for reconciliation. Letting go of expectations allows parents to focus on loving freely, without the emotional burden of needing their child to respond in a specific way.

This doesn't mean giving up hope for the future—it means freeing yourself from the need for validation. It is an act of loving with the understanding that reconciliation, if it happens, will come when the time is right, and on the child's terms. In the meantime, parents can continue to express love without the need for reciprocity.

3. **Creating Emotional Space for Love**: Practicing unconditional love requires emotional resilience. Parents must find ways to keep their hearts open, even when they are hurt, and to continue offering love without expecting it to be returned. This involves cultivating self-compassion and resilience—by acknowledging the pain of estrangement, while also creating space for love to exist.

Parents may need to establish emotional boundaries that prevent the estrangement from becoming a source of constant emotional turmoil. This doesn't mean shutting off love, but instead creating room for emotional healing and self-care, while still holding space for the child in their hearts.

Rituals, Prayers, and Quiet Acts of Continued Care

When communication is limited or absent, parents may feel helpless, unsure of how to continue showing love to their child. However, there are many ways to practice continued care through rituals, prayers, and small acts that affirm your love and commitment, even when physical contact isn't possible.

1. **Rituals of Remembrance**: One of the most powerful ways to stay connected to love without direct contact is through rituals of remembrance. These can be simple, daily practices that remind you of your child, your love for them, and your ongoing hopes for their well-being. These rituals can be comforting acts that bring you peace, while also serving as a silent offering of love to your child.

   o **Lighting a candle**: A simple ritual such as lighting a candle for your child each day can symbolize your ongoing connection. As the candle burns, it can represent your love, your hopes for reconciliation, and the warmth that you continue to offer them, even from a distance.

   o **Creating a memory altar**: Some parents create a small altar or space of remembrance, where they place meaningful objects, photographs, or mementos that connect them to their child. This can be a powerful way to honor the love you have for them, while also providing a space for reflection and prayer.

○ **Anniversary rituals**: On significant dates—birthdays, holidays, or the anniversary of the estrangement—performing a ritual such as writing a letter, saying a prayer, or taking a walk in their memory can provide a sense of connection. These rituals help to honor your relationship and acknowledge your child's presence in your heart, even if they are not physically present.

2. **Prayers and Affirmations**: For many parents, prayer can be a powerful tool for staying connected to their child in times of estrangement. Prayer is an expression of hope, care, and love that transcends physical distance. Whether through formal prayers or personal affirmations, parents can offer their child thoughts of love, healing, and protection.

○ **Praying for healing**: Parents can pray for the emotional healing of their child, for their peace of mind, and for eventual reconciliation, if that is in alignment with both parties' desires. These prayers are a way to continue caring for their child's well-being, even when direct contact is not possible.

○ **Affirmations of love**: Daily affirmations—statements of unconditional love, support, and forgiveness—can help parents stay grounded in their desire to maintain connection. These affirmations can be simple, such as, "I love you no matter where you are," or "I trust that healing will come in time." Repeating these affirmations helps parents release the grip of pain and reconnect with the power of unconditional love.

3. **Quiet Acts of Continued Care**: Even when estranged, there are small, quiet acts of care that parents can offer to their child, whether they are aware of them or not. This could be something as simple as offering a prayer for their safety, sending a small gift or letter without expecting a response, or donating to a cause that was important to them. These acts are not about trying to manipulate or force reconciliation, but rather about continuing to honor the relationship through gestures of love and care.

   o **Sending something meaningful**: While it can be painful to send something without receiving a response, offering a gift or card that reflects your child's interests or needs (perhaps a favorite book, a meaningful object, or a simple note) can be an act of love. If there is no response, it's important to understand that the act itself— offering love and care—is enough. The child's journey and timeline for reconciliation are beyond your control, but the love you offer remains constant.

   o **Volunteering in their name**: If your child is passionate about a particular cause, one quiet way of showing love is by volunteering or donating to that cause in their name. This can be a way to honor their values and offer continued care, even when direct contact is not possible.

Love That Expects Nothing in Return – But Always Leaves the Light On

Perhaps the most powerful expression of love during estrangement is the love that expects nothing in return but always leaves the light on. This is the love that is unconditional and unshakeable, one that does not demand reconciliation or communication, but simply waits with an open heart. It is a love that says, "I am here, whenever you are ready," without pressing for immediate resolution.

1. **Embracing the Concept of Unconditional Love**: The most profound aspect of this love is that it does not demand or expect anything in return. It's a love that doesn't seek validation, recognition, or immediate acknowledgment—it simply exists. This can be an incredibly freeing concept for estranged parents to embrace. You no longer need to pressure yourself to "fix" things or force reconciliation; you can simply allow love to flow freely from your heart, knowing that it is enough in and of itself.

2. **Leaving the Light On**: The metaphor of "leaving the light on" symbolizes an open, welcoming heart that is always ready to receive. It is about keeping the door of love ajar, even in the face of estrangement. While this metaphor doesn't mean waiting passively or with a sense of desperation, it does convey the idea that the possibility of reconnection is always there, grounded in love. The light is always on, signaling that the love remains constant, no matter how much time passes.

Example: If your child reaches out in the future, even after years of silence, your response is a reflection of the enduring love you have always carried. You can respond with kindness, respect, and understanding, knowing that your love has remained a steady, guiding force throughout the estrangement. The light was never extinguished—it was simply waiting for the right moment to shine again.

3. **Acceptance Without Attachment**: The love that expects nothing in return is not attached to any particular outcome. It is rooted in the understanding that love is a gift in itself, and that the act of loving is as meaningful as the potential for reconciliation. Estranged parents can find peace by embracing this type of love—one that is freely given and unconditionally offered, without expectation of what it will bring.

Conclusion

Estrangement can be an incredibly painful and isolating experience, but the love that persists through distance is a testament to the strength and resilience of the human heart. Parents who love their children even without contact have the opportunity to practice a form of love that is truly unconditional—one that transcends time, space, and the need for reciprocation. Through rituals, prayers, and quiet acts of care, parents can continue to nurture that love, even in the absence of physical presence or communication.

Ultimately, love that expects nothing in return but always leaves the light on is the purest form of connection. It is a love that honors the other person's journey, accepts the reality of estrangement, and remains steadfast in its presence. Whether reconciliation occurs in the future or not, this love is a powerful force that shapes the parent's journey toward healing and peace. It is a love that never falters, and it is always there— waiting, hopeful, and unwavering.

Chapter 12

Helping Others Understand – Navigating Judgment and Isolation

Introduction

Estrangement is often a deeply personal and isolating experience, one that can be complicated by societal judgments and misunderstandings. Parents who are estranged from their children often find themselves in an emotionally charged space, not only dealing with the pain of separation but also navigating the reactions of friends, family, and society at large. There is a stigma attached to estrangement that can make parents feel ashamed, misunderstood, and alone. The pressure to explain, justify, or defend their situation can feel overwhelming, especially when the outside world doesn't understand the complexities of the estranged relationship.

In this chapter, we will explore how estranged parents can deal with societal shame and misunderstanding, how to respond to awkward questions and "helpful" advice from others, and the importance of joining or creating support groups for estranged parents. This chapter aims to help parents regain their sense of agency and self-worth in the face of external judgment, offering tools for managing conversations and seeking out community support during one of the most difficult times in their lives.

Dealing with Societal Shame and Misunderstanding

Estranged parents often face judgment from family members, friends, and society, who may fail to grasp the complexities of the situation. The perception that "good" parents don't become estranged from their children is pervasive, and parents may be met with harsh criticism or even shunning when the estrangement is revealed. This can amplify the feelings of shame and guilt, making the healing process even more challenging.

1. **The Stigma of Estrangement**: There is a cultural narrative that associates good parenting with continuous closeness and harmony. When estranged parents reveal their situation, they may be made to feel as though they are failures, blamed for the breakdown of the relationship, or viewed as being at fault. This societal expectation can make estranged parents feel alienated, as though their pain is misunderstood or dismissed. In many cases, people may judge parents without understanding the full story— overlooking the nuances of the estranged relationship, the child's needs, or the history of the situation.

   One of the first steps in navigating this shame is to understand that societal expectations about parenthood are often unrealistic. Good parents are not immune to complex, difficult relationships with their children. Estrangement happens for a variety of reasons—some within the parent's control, others outside of it— and it does not diminish the value of the love and effort a parent has invested. It is important to hold on to the understanding that your worth as a person is not defined by your relationship with your child.

2. **Releasing the Shame**: The shame of estrangement can be deeply ingrained, but it is essential for estranged parents to release this burden. Parents may feel ashamed of their perceived failure, but it's important to recognize that estrangement is a complex, multifaceted experience. It is not always a result of neglect, abuse, or poor parenting; sometimes, it arises from miscommunication, personal differences, or emotional struggles on both sides.

   In releasing the shame, it's helpful to remember that no one can fully understand the nuances of a family relationship from the outside. Societal norms may place pressure on parents to maintain certain images of family unity, but this does not reflect the reality of every family's situation. Accepting that estrangement is not a reflection of your inherent worth as a parent or as a person is key to moving forward and healing.

3. **Finding Inner Validation**: One of the most powerful ways to navigate societal judgment is by seeking validation from within. It's essential to acknowledge your pain, your efforts, and your commitment to the relationship with your child, even if that relationship is strained or distant. Remind yourself that, no matter what others may say or think, you know the truth of your experience. Inner validation involves accepting that you are doing the best you can in a difficult situation and that your feelings, needs, and boundaries are legitimate. By grounding yourself in

your own sense of worth, you can begin to deflect external judgment and focus on your emotional well-being.

How to Respond to Awkward Questions and "Helpful" Advice

As an estranged parent, you will likely encounter awkward questions, unsolicited advice, and misguided comments from others who are uncomfortable with the estrangement. These interactions can be painful, frustrating, and emotionally taxing. While you are under no obligation to explain your situation to others, knowing how to respond—or when to simply set boundaries—can help alleviate some of the stress that comes with these encounters.

1. **Dealing with Awkward Questions**: Estranged parents often encounter questions that feel invasive or judgmental. Family members or friends may ask, "What happened between you two?" or "Have you tried reaching out?" While these questions may come from a place of concern or curiosity, they can feel like pressure to explain or justify the estrangement.

   o **How to Respond**: One way to respond is to simply acknowledge the difficulty of the situation without going into specifics. For example, you might say, "This is a really hard situation for me, and I'm still processing it. I appreciate your concern, but I'd rather not discuss the details right now." This sets a boundary without feeling the need to explain or justify yourself.

○ Another response could be, "I'm not ready to talk about it, but thank you for caring." This provides a polite yet firm way of letting others know that the topic is off-limits, without feeling pressured to provide more information than you are comfortable with.

2. **Navigating Unsolicited "Helpful" Advice**: People often feel compelled to offer solutions or "helpful" advice when they are uncomfortable with someone else's pain. Estranged parents may hear suggestions such as, "You should just call them," or "Why don't you go visit them?" While well-intentioned, such advice can feel dismissive of the complexities of the situation and may increase the sense of frustration or powerlessness.

○ **How to Respond**: A gentle, yet firm response could be, "I appreciate your suggestion, but I've already considered many options. Right now, I'm focusing on healing and respecting my child's space." This approach acknowledges the advice without taking it on as your own responsibility. Alternatively, you might say, "I know you want to help, and I'm doing the best I can in a very difficult situation. I'd appreciate your support as I navigate it."

3. **Setting Boundaries Around Unwanted Conversations**: If certain individuals continually press for details or offer advice that feels overwhelming or inappropriate, it's important to set clear boundaries. A simple, respectful response like, "I'm not

ready to talk about it in detail, but thank you for respecting my privacy," can help maintain emotional safety. Setting these boundaries will empower you to protect yourself emotionally while still maintaining respect for others' curiosity or concern.

4. **Understanding That Others May Not Understand**: Ultimately, it's important to recognize that others may not fully grasp the intricacies of estrangement. Their discomfort with the situation may manifest in intrusive questions or unsolicited advice, and they may not understand why you are not ready to talk about it. This lack of understanding is not a reflection of your worth or your experience, but simply a result of the limited perspective they have on your situation. While their reactions can be hurtful, it's essential to maintain compassion for their ignorance and stay focused on your own healing process.

Joining or Creating Support Groups for Estranged Parents

One of the most valuable ways to navigate the isolation of estrangement is by joining or creating support groups for estranged parents. These groups provide a space for parents to share their experiences, find solace in the company of others who understand, and receive guidance on how to cope with the emotional and societal challenges of estrangement.

1. **The Benefits of Support Groups**: Estranged parents often feel isolated, as few people outside of the experience truly understand the pain and complexities of estrangement. Support groups

provide a safe, non-judgmental environment where parents can share their struggles, exchange coping strategies, and find comfort in knowing that they are not alone. Being in a group of people who truly understand can be healing and validating, as it provides a space for emotional release and connection.

- o **Emotional Support**: Support groups allow parents to share their feelings of grief, frustration, and loss with others who are experiencing similar emotions. This can provide a sense of relief and help alleviate the feelings of isolation that often accompany estrangement.

- o **Practical Guidance**: Many support groups also offer practical advice for coping with estrangement, including ways to manage emotional triggers, how to respond to difficult situations, and suggestions for navigating the complexities of the estranged relationship.

2. **Creating Your Own Support Group**: If you are unable to find a support group in your area, consider creating one. This can be done through online platforms, such as Facebook or specialized forums, or through local community organizations. Creating a space for estranged parents to connect can help foster a sense of belonging and provide a valuable outlet for sharing experiences and resources.

- o **Online Communities**: In the digital age, online communities provide a convenient way to connect with others who understand your experience, no matter where you live. Online forums and Facebook groups dedicated to estranged parents allow for a sense of community without geographic limitations. These virtual spaces can provide a valuable support network and allow you to share and receive advice from people who are going through similar experiences.

○ **Local In-Person Groups**: For those who prefer in-person support, consider reaching out to local therapists or support organizations that specialize in family dynamics or estrangement. They may have groups or resources specifically for estranged parents. If none exist, you might consider organizing a small, informal group where parents can meet in person to discuss their experiences and offer mutual support.

Conclusion

Estrangement can be one of the most isolating experiences a parent can go through, but navigating the judgment, misunderstanding, and isolation from others doesn't have to be done alone. By recognizing the societal stigma and shame surrounding estrangement and developing strategies for dealing with awkward questions and unsolicited advice, estranged parents can protect their emotional well-being and assert control over their journey. Additionally, joining or creating support groups can provide a much-needed sense of community, validation, and understanding from others who have lived through similar challenges.

The journey through estrangement requires immense emotional resilience, but it also offers the opportunity to connect with others who understand, to redefine personal boundaries, and to reclaim your sense of self-worth. By prioritizing your own healing and finding support, you can navigate the societal pressures and emotional isolation of estrangement with strength, dignity, and a renewed sense of hope.

Chapter 13

Your Life, Still Beautiful – Peace, Meaning, and the Long View

Introduction

Estrangement can leave an indelible mark on a parent's heart and mind, shaping their journey in ways they never expected. Yet, as with all forms of profound loss, there is space within that heartache for healing, growth, and beauty. It may seem counterintuitive to speak of beauty in the wake of estrangement, but when grief and joy coexist, something remarkable happens. The scars left behind by such a painful chapter in life can give rise to a deeper understanding of peace, strength, and purpose. And over time, the journey may teach you more about grace, endurance, and the resilience of the human spirit than you could ever imagine.

In this chapter, we will explore how grief and joy can exist side by side, how your journey can serve as a testament to grace and endurance, and how embracing the fullness of life—including its scars and struggles—can lead to peace, meaning, and a profound appreciation for the beauty of your existence. This is not a chapter about the absence of pain, but about finding the beauty and purpose in life, even after the most painful of experiences.

Grief and Joy Can Coexist

One of the most profound lessons of estrangement is learning that grief and joy are not mutually exclusive. In fact, they often coexist in a delicate dance, each enriching and deepening the other. It is easy to assume that joy can only exist in the absence of pain, or that healing means the complete elimination of sorrow. However, true healing and growth come from the recognition that grief and joy can exist together, creating a complex but beautiful tapestry of experience.

1. **The Depth of Grief**: Estrangement brings with it profound sorrow—a loss that cannot be fully understood unless experienced. It is the loss of a relationship, the loss of expectations, and the loss of the vision of what family life was supposed to be. This grief is real, and it is important to acknowledge it fully. But part of the healing process involves accepting that grief will not forever define you. It may shape you, but it does not have to limit your capacity to experience joy in other areas of life.

2. **The Presence of Joy**: Joy may feel distant or elusive during the depths of estrangement, but it can return, often in unexpected ways. It might come through small moments of personal achievement, through the love and connection you share with others, or through the rediscovery of hobbies or passions that had been set aside. Joy does not invalidate the grief you carry; instead, it offers a counterbalance, reminding you that life is still full of beauty, even amid sorrow.

Example: You might find joy in the laughter of a friend, the warmth of a family gathering, or the quiet peace that comes with a solitary walk in nature. These moments of joy are not about forgetting the pain of estrangement; they are about affirming that life is still full of moments worth celebrating, even when you are grieving.

3. **The Integration of Grief and Joy**: Over time, grief and joy begin to integrate into a more complex and richer understanding of life. The grief you carry does not diminish the joy you can experience; rather, it enhances your appreciation for life's fleeting moments of beauty. You learn to live in the present, understanding that the pain of estrangement is part of your story, but it does not define the entirety of your existence.

Embracing the coexistence of grief and joy means allowing yourself the freedom to feel both, without judgment. You do not have to choose one over the other. Your grief, in fact, gives depth to your joy, and your joy gives you the strength to carry your grief.

What Your Journey Teaches Others About Grace and Endurance

Your journey of estrangement, with all its pain, struggle, and uncertainty, holds lessons of grace and endurance that can inspire others. As you navigate the highs and lows of healing, you may find that your story is a testament to the human capacity for resilience, compassion, and hope. While estrangement can feel like an isolating experience, it is also a deeply human one, and it teaches lessons that resonate with many.

4. **The Power of Grace**: Grace is the ability to maintain compassion and kindness, even in the face of deep hurt. It is the capacity to forgive—not necessarily the other person, but yourself and the circumstances that led to estrangement. As you move through the pain of estrangement, you may find that grace becomes one of your greatest allies. It is the grace to accept the reality of your situation without judgment, the grace to forgive yourself for what you perceive as mistakes, and the grace to remain open to future possibilities, even if they seem distant.

Your journey teaches others that grace is not about perfection, but about compassion in the face of imperfection. It is about accepting life's difficulties and responding with empathy—not just to others, but to yourself. By living with grace, you demonstrate that it is possible to navigate hardship with dignity and kindness, even when life feels overwhelmingly painful.

5. **Endurance Through Adversity**: Endurance is the quiet strength that allows you to keep going even when the road ahead is unclear. Estrangement tests endurance in ways that many other experiences do not. It requires a patience that comes from deep within, a commitment to continue forward despite the emotional toll. But it is through this endurance that you discover your own resilience—the ability to rise again after each setback, to continue loving and living fully, even in the face of hardship.

Your journey teaches others that endurance is not about pushing through without rest, but about accepting the pace of healing and honoring the process. It is a slow and steady approach to life, one that prioritizes self-care, growth, and the recognition that healing is not linear. Endurance teaches us that, although the journey is long, it is also full of lessons and rewards that only become evident over time.

6. **Inspiring Others**: The way you handle estrangement—whether you share your story with others or simply live your life with resilience and compassion—can inspire those around you. Your ability to navigate this painful experience with grace and endurance demonstrates to others that it is possible to live through hardship and emerge with a greater sense of strength, purpose, and love. Whether or not you choose to talk about your experience openly, your actions, your resilience, and your capacity to move forward will show others the power of grace and endurance.

Embracing Life Fully – Scars, Strength, and All

One of the most profound realizations that comes with estrangement is that life continues, even in the aftermath of deep pain. While the scars of estrangement may never fully fade, they become part of your story—shaping you, yes, but also giving you a depth of experience that allows you to embrace life more fully. You may never "go back" to the person you were before estrangement, but you can move forward with strength, compassion, and a new perspective on what truly matters.

1. **The Beauty of Scars**: Scars are often seen as marks of injury or imperfection, but they also symbolize healing and growth. Each

scar tells a story of endurance, of pain that has been overcome, and of resilience in the face of hardship. As you move through the process of healing from estrangement, you will undoubtedly carry scars—emotional reminders of the loss and the journey. But these scars are also a testament to your ability to survive and grow. They are evidence of the strength you have cultivated, even in the face of the most challenging circumstances.

Embrace your scars as part of your unique story. They do not diminish your beauty; they add to it. Your scars are symbols of the love you gave, the pain you endured, and the wisdom you gained.

2. **The Strength Within**: As you navigate the complexities of estrangement, you will discover an inner strength you may not have known you had. The journey requires you to tap into deep reserves of resilience, patience, and emotional endurance. Each time you rise after a setback, each time you choose healing over despair, you strengthen your capacity to face life's challenges with greater fortitude. This strength will serve you not only in navigating estrangement but in every area of your life.

   Strength is not about toughness or resistance; it is about the ability to bend without breaking, to weather the storms of life and emerge still standing, still compassionate, and still open to the possibilities ahead.

3. **Living Fully, Despite Pain**: Embracing life fully doesn't mean pretending that everything is perfect. It means acknowledging the

pain of estrangement, allowing yourself to grieve, but also choosing to live with intention, joy, and meaning. It's about finding moments of beauty, connection, and fulfillment, even while carrying the weight of the past. Life, with all its complexities, still holds the possibility of joy, growth, and love.

Living fully means embracing your life—scars, strength, and all—knowing that you are more than your pain. You are more than your role as a parent. You are a person with dreams, desires, and the capacity for joy, and you have the power to create a life filled with meaning, even in the face of difficulty.

Conclusion

Your journey of estrangement is one that brings pain, but it also brings wisdom, strength, and beauty. The coexistence of grief and joy, the grace and endurance you demonstrate, and the scars you carry are all part of the intricate fabric of your life. Through the process of healing, you have discovered that life does not stop with hardship—it transforms you, deepens you, and offers new opportunities for growth and meaning.

As you continue on this journey, know that your life is still beautiful. Your capacity for love, resilience, and joy remains intact, and your story is one that speaks of endurance, grace, and the power of the human spirit. Embrace your life fully, knowing that, even with scars, you are more whole, more connected, and more capable of embracing the beauty of existence than ever before.

Epilogue

In *Life After Estrangement: A Guide for Parents Cut Off by Adult Children*, we have journeyed together through the complexities of estrangement—an often misunderstood and unspoken pain that parents endure when their adult children cut ties. The emotional toll of estrangement is far-reaching, deeply affecting parental identity, emotional well-being, and the family dynamics that once seemed secure. This book has illuminated the nuances of this loss, helping parents understand that estrangement is not just an absence but a profound, ambiguous loss that can challenge their sense of self and purpose. We've explored how estrangement can silently shape a life, leaving deep scars that require compassion, understanding, and time to heal.

As we've discussed throughout the chapters, estrangement is rarely the result of a single event but rather the culmination of multiple factors: misunderstood boundaries, unresolved trauma, generational patterns, and shifting societal values around autonomy and self-care. While the rise of estrangement may seem disheartening, it is important to remember that it reflects broader cultural shifts—shifting views on family, personal well-being, and the changing definitions of what constitutes a "healthy" relationship. The book's exploration of these social dynamics offers estranged parents clarity, helping them understand that they are not alone in this experience.

The emotional landscape of estrangement is tumultuous and often overwhelming. In Chapter 4, we explored the rollercoaster of emotions—guilt, shame, anger, and sadness—that estranged parents navigate. These feelings, while normal, can be paralyzing if not processed in healthy ways. We've offered strategies for emotional healing, such as journaling, therapy, and allowing space for these emotions without letting them control our lives. In Chapter 5, we shifted from self-blame to self-compassion, encouraging parents to reframe their story—not as a narrative of failure but one of human complexity, where everyone involved was doing the best they could with the circumstances they were given. This reframing is crucial for reclaiming personal peace and releasing the need for perfection.

We also explored the art of letting go—a delicate balance between detaching with grace and holding on to love. As we discussed in Chapter 6, letting go doesn't mean giving up or withdrawing affection. Instead, it's about releasing the need for control and trusting that love can persist, even from a distance. It's about honoring personal boundaries while maintaining an open heart, and this mindset is a crucial step towards inner peace.

Throughout the book, we've learned that estrangement doesn't define you as a parent or as a person. In Chapter 9, we emphasized the importance of reclaiming your identity beyond the role of a parent, rediscovering your passions, and finding meaning outside of familial relationships. This chapter was about embracing your wholeness as a human being—whether that means nurturing friendships, delving into hobbies, or finding a spiritual connection that offers peace. Estrangement may have altered your path, but it does not erase your worth or the beauty of your life.

When estrangement ends, if it does, reconciliation is never a return to the past, but rather an opportunity to create something new. In Chapter 10, we discussed the fragile nature of reconciliation, understanding that trust-building is a delicate process and that boundaries may evolve. Reuniting does not mean going back to how things were—it means finding a way to coexist with the new version of the relationship, one that is rooted in respect, understanding, and careful navigation of new boundaries.

For those who continue to face estrangement, staying connected to love from a distance is an ongoing practice. In Chapter 11, we highlighted how to keep the light on—whether through quiet acts of care, rituals, or simply holding space for unconditional love. Estranged parents can still practice compassion, even without contact, knowing that their love remains a constant, enduring force in their lives.

Helping others understand the experience of estrangement is another important aspect of healing. In Chapter 12, we addressed the societal shame and judgment that estranged parents often face and provided strategies for managing these difficult interactions. By joining support groups or creating spaces where estranged parents can connect, we provide each other with validation, empathy, and solidarity—a reminder that we are not alone in this journey.

Finally, in Chapter 13, we discussed how estrangement is a chapter in your life, not the final word. It is a journey of grief and growth, where joy and sorrow can coexist. As you move forward, your story becomes a source of strength and grace. The long view teaches you that despite the scars, life can still be beautiful. You can emerge from the pain not as a victim of estrangement, but as someone who has endured, grown, and embraced life with renewed strength, compassion, and hope.

The path after estrangement is one of resilience, transformation, and the quiet power of letting go without giving up hope. This book has been a roadmap for navigating that path with dignity and grace, and it's my hope that, as you walk this journey, you continue to find peace, healing, and a deep connection to the love that resides within you.

www.ingramcontent.com/pod-product-compliance
Lightning Source LLC
Chambersburg PA
CBHW071523120626
46550CB00006B/2342